A POWERFUL STORY OF MYSTICISM AND LOVE—
NOW A MAJOR FILM FROM EMBASSY PICTURES

He was seven years old when he disappeared from the Amazon damsite where his father, an American construction engineer, was at work.

For ten years, the father spent every spare moment searching for his son. But when they met again, the boy knew only one father, the chief of the primitive Indian tribe called the "Invisible People." . . .

So begins the adventure of THE EMERALD FOREST, a story of the mystical power of the vast Amazon rain forest and the bonds of human love. Based on a true story, it is now a major family/adventure film directed by John Boorman.

INCLUDES COLOR PHOTOS AND
A SPECIAL POSTSCRIPT ON THE MAKING OF
"THE EMERALD FOREST"

THE EMERALD FOREST

Robert Holdstock was born in 1948, in Kent, the eldest of five children. He read Zoology at the University College of North Wales, then Medical Zoology at the London School of Hygiene, where he gained an M.Sc.

Writing fiction, especially science-fiction and supernatural stories, has been a hobby since the age of nine. His first stories were published in the late 1960's. In 1975 his first novel appeared and in the same year he abandoned medicine to become a freelance writer. Since that time he has written over twenty books, including television novelizations, occult tales (*Necromancer* and *Night Hunter*), muscular historical fantasies (*The Berserker*) and science fiction, including *Eye Among the Blind, Earthwind* and *Where Time Winds Blow*. In collaboration he has produced five large-format, illustrated books, including *Alien Landscapes, Tour of the Universe* and *Lost Realms of Fantasy*. His most recent novel is *Mythago Wood*, a fantasy about the genesis of myth and myth figures in our history. It won the British Science Fiction Association's Award in 1985. A sequel, *Lavondyss*, is in preparation.

JOHN BOORMAN'S

THE EMERALD FOREST

THE EMERALD FOREST is set in a version of Garamond. Typesetting was done by Crane Typesetting Services, Inc. The book was printed and bound by Maple-Vail Book Manufacturing Group at their York, PA plant.

Cover design: Jo Imeson

Chapter Logotype: Susan Schenker

John Boorman's
THE EMERALD FOREST
Novel by Robert Holdstock
based on a screenplay by Rospo Pallenberg

Library of Congress Cataloging in Publication Number: 85-061547

ISBN 0-918432-70-7

New York Zoetrope
80 East 11th Street
New York, NY 10003

Printed in the United States of America
First Printing: June, 1985
5 4 3

JOHN BOORMAN'S

THE EMERALD FOREST

By Robert Holdstock
Based on a screenplay by
Rospo Pallenberg

New York Zoetrope

CONTENTS

'We will always be in the forest.
Even though you believe we are not in the forest,
we will be there.
You will just not see us.
Because you do not know how *to see us.'*
—Wai-wai saying

PROLOGUE

Years later, when the memories of what he had left behind had become just ghosts, he would still remember the time of his first loneliness, the sadness and the loss that had blanketed his senses for so many months.

At these times he would journey alone to the edge of the world and stand, half in, half out of the forest, one side of his body in the warm gloom, the other in the bright sunshine. And he would sway between the worlds as he had swayed between them as a child; only then, in those days, he had been gripping the end of a liana, draped from the high branch of a tree, and his father had been pushing him.

It was good to shed tears during his time at the edge of the world. He was an old man, now, and the ghosts of the two worlds followed him. With each tear would come a memory, usually the echo of ancient laughter, and sometimes he could not tell from which world the laughter came. So he would leave the edge of the world and make the long trek home to his family. Somehow the journey was all he needed to banish the shadows of grief. Somehow, too, his mind would fill with new stories, and when his grandchildren clustered around him, he would sit them down in a tight circle and speak to them in the hushed, eerie voice that so scared and enthralled them.

His stories, now, were all about the dreamlight, but at the core of them were the images that were his last remembered ghosts. There was the story of the "man who ran into the World and could not see the people there," and the image for this was of a man running across a dry field, his limbs waving like a pelican attempting flight; his mouth was open, his head thrown back, and the air was loud with his shout. And, as if in a strange, slow dream, the man never reached the forest, but continued to run towards it, howling out his haunting cry.

Then there was the story of the "room in the great stone tree," and the image for this was of a man climbing one of the stone trees that grew in the wilderness, peering into the bright light of a room carved into its top, where people sat round a table and looked at images of the spirits of the dead.

But his favorite stories were always those he told about the Dead Forest. He would save them until last, because they were the most frightening, and very often by the time he had finished speaking *all* the family were sitting round, and not just the children.

He had many stories of the Dead Forest. But they all began in the same way, and they were all based on the same remembered image, of a boy alone in a strange land.

At a time, in that place beyond the edge of the world, there was a boy who walked through the stone trees of the Dead Forest. And all around him there were people, but the people spoke strange words, and he could not understand them . . .

PART ONE

The Wilderness

1

He had *tried* to learn the language! But he was only seven, and Portuguese was one of the most difficult tongues to learn; it was not a bit like English, despite what his father had said about the two languages having much in common.

Tommy Markham stood, half in, half out of the tall, lush green vegetation that grew at the edge of the playground. He watched the local kids as they played on the metal structures of the adventure park, and felt deep envy of the fun they were having. It was a hot, sticky day and his shirt was uncomfortable. Each of the game structures seemed to be owned by one or two bigger children, who only allowed their friends to play. They shouted and yelled, and they laughed, but although Tommy recognized the occasional word he might as well have been on another planet.

The Markham family hadn't even been here a day yet, and already Tommy was missing his friends in Newbury, California. And they were going to be here for so long! So many years. Why couldn't the engineers build dams in just a few weeks? Why did it have to take so long? By the time they got back to Lincoln Avenue, in Newbury, all his friends would have grown up and gone away, and he'd be so old that no new kids would want to talk to him.

Brazil was definitely *bad news*.

Gloomily, he stepped away from the obscuring growth at the playground's edge and walked cautiously across the patterned concrete ground. He longed to be sharing in the games, he longed to know what the sunburnt kids were shouting and saying. One of them came up to him and stared at him hard, a confident grin on his face. "*Que cabelo louro*!" he said, and laughed. As Tommy walked past him the playground echoed to the taunting cry: "*Estrangeiro*! *Estrangeiro louro*!"

He looked different. Even the American children in the nearby market, where his mother was still shopping, even they were suntanned and swarthy, now. Tommy's skin was as white as snow, and his blond hair, an unruly mass that curled to his shoulders, set him even further apart. As the dark eyes of the local children watched him, he stared back through eyes of the clearest, brightest blue.

The city was called Belore. It was two hundred miles inland from the Brazilian coast, built along a leisurely curve of the Yuruan River, which was itself a tributary of the giant Amazon. The river was Belore's main connection with other towns in this South American land; there were three highways, too, and Tommy had seen them from the plane, great slashes of red across the grey-green landscape.

On the other side of the water, the jungle began. It was not *really* jungle, Tommy knew. There were farmers there, and foresters, and tribes that traded with the city, and priests, and oilmen . . .

But deeper in that forest there were Indians.

Indians!

In a way, Tommy felt let down. His father had tantalized him with tales of the real, honest-to-God Indians who still lived in the forest. Instead of learning Portuguese, Tommy had spent his preparation evenings fantasizing about what they would look like, how the air would be filled with the sound of their drums, and the smell of their peace pipes.

His "research" into the Indians of the Amazon Basin had been as lazy and as hasty as any research designed *not* to learn the reality, only to sustain the imagination.

He had come to Belore expecting something akin to the Wild West. The only Indians he had seen, so far, had missing teeth, wrinkled skins, and wore baggy shirts and trousers. They had watched him, as the Markham family had walked through Belore's shanty town, with an indifference matched exactly by his own disappointment.

His father had *tricked* him.

"Belore is beautiful, Tommy," his father had said. "It's so colorful, it's like living in the *National Geographic* magazine. It makes Newbury look like Tombstone. You're going to love it. It's hot, good river swimming, great food, the kids are bright, the girls are *great* . . ." father-to-son nudging, the broadest of winks. "And there are *Indians*. A hundred miles from the city it's like stepping back into time. You're going to *love* it, Tommy."

"Do they have electricity in Belore?"

"Sure they have electricity. They'll have even more when the dam's built."

"Do they have TV?"

"Of course. Where do you think we're going? The South Pole?"

"Do they have McDonalds?"

"I sure as hell hope so, son."

After a pause: "Okay. It's a deal. You go. I'll come too."

2

Their first day in Belore was chaos. Jean spent over an hour trying to make contact with the Belore and District Children's Foundation, where she would be teaching, but no one answered the phone. She went shopping in the market, Tommy and Heather in tow, and nearly died when Tommy wandered off into the playground and she lost him for a few minutes. Heather had toothache, but it was one of her "punishment" toothaches that came on when she was forbidden to play with certain things that fascinated her: in this case a large, red-backed bug that had been sunning itself on the plants of the apartment's balcony.

Bill Markham had hoped for a few days to settle in before his first meeting with the AmazCo Corporation, who were building the dam up-river. "Just an hour," his immediate senior on the project—Enrico Costa—had begged. That hour, thanks to the thoughtless demands of the Project Supervisor, Joseph Perrera, had stretched to six. When he finally got home—as much as the crate-infested apartment could yet be called home—he discovered an atmosphere of minor rebellion.

It was late afternoon. Jean was still trying to make contact with her people. The food for the evening meal was neatly cut and ready for the two of them to cook. Heather was sitting at a packing case, a large book of exotic insects open upon it, her face in her hands. Absorbed.

"Where's Tommy?"

Jean placed the phone back on the hook and shook her head with exasperation. She looked exhausted. Her fair hair was a series of anguish-induced spikes about her head. Her thin face looked more pinched than usual. "Tommy? He's out on the balcony. What took you so long?"

"They're glad to have me. Couldn't get away." Bill shrugged off his jacket and loosened his tie. Smart suits seemed out of character for the man. He was dark complexioned and muscular. He felt—and looked—more comfortable in a tracksuit.

"You should have taken the kids . . ." Jean said.

"I know. I'm sorry. But I didn't think I'd be more than a few minutes. I'm treading carefully—those guys are big business."

"*All* of this is big business," Jean said. Bill smiled and the two of them hugged, weary from travel, overwhelmed by the amount of sorting out to do, desperate for a time of quiet together, a time to talk.

"You've had a pretty tough first day too, by the looks of it," Bill said.

"You could say that. And when you've said it, say it again. No one answers the phone. They argue with you in the market. And Tommy isn't exactly the sunshine kid of the year."

"He'll get used to Belore. Just like we all will."

Jean tugged away from him. "Well, go and have a word with him. He's missed you."

Tommy was kneeling at the balcony rail, the family's large Zeiss binoculars clutched firmly in his hands. Even so, the binoculars wavered precariously and Bill reached out to the leather strap, looping it over his son's head.

"What can you see?"

"The river," Tommy said.

Bill crouched down by the boy. "What else?"

"The forest. You can't see much. Just trees."

"No Indians, huh?"

"Not yet."

Bill let his gaze drift over the city. It was dusk but the light was unlike anything he had ever seen before. They were looking to the west, across the shanty town that had grown along the river, away from the main harbor. Nearer, the city was as bustling and as modern as any city, with rooftop gardens and huge statuary, and black marble façades to the high-rise offices; and of course, a spill of bright night life in the tourist sectors.

The shanty town was like a place of ghosts, a dark, forbidding strip in which cold lights burned. The river beyond was already giving off the mist that so often shrouded it from dusk until dawn, so that the sheer edge of the jungle beyond was now grey, all color lost.

Bill took the binoculars from his son. He scanned the far side of the river. Lights burned in the huts and shacks along the bank. To the south the land was cleared and the jungle that he now contemplated was in fact the home of many farmers and loggers and itinerants, content to exist at the interzone between the worlds. It amazed him, though, to see how strong, how forbidding that forest looked. As if, despite its occupation and use by the Brazilians and those half-castes who would never live in towns or cities, as if, despite all of these, it clung to an identity that at dusk showed it in its full and sinister light.

He turned the glasses, scanning the high-rise heart of the city. The AmazCo building was a slender finger, higher than the surrounding structures, its nature brightly signalled in glowing red letters.

Bill gave the glasses back to his son. He helped the boy train them on the building. "That's where I'll be working a lot of the time," he said.

"I'll be able to watch you," Tommy said.

"But a lot more of the time I'll be way out there, beyond the tree line."

Tommy stared into the grey distance. His breathing was steady, and Bill watched him, aware that the boy's interest was slowly rising. It would only be a matter of days before he accepted the new locale. Tommy was so old for his age, but then so was Heather. Kids seemed sharper, these days, the diet of fast TV making them more aware. In Newbury, Tommy had formed the sort of relationships with kids of his own age that a generation before had not formed until a child was ten or eleven.

Bill Markham suddenly realized that his son had his eyes closed and was whispering inaudibly as he faced the distance.

"What's that all about?"

Without opening his eyes, Tommy said, "I'm calling them."

"Calling who?"

"The Indians. The Indians you said lived in the jungle. I'm calling them, like Charlie X."

"Who's Charlie X?"

"On *Star Trek*. He could call people with his mind."

Bill smiled. "Well, don't call them too hard." He surreptitiously encircled Tommy with his arms, then grabbed the boy. "They might come *creeping* into the *apartment*!"

Tommy yelled and laughed, struggling in his father's tormentingly ticklish embrace.

Then there was a strange sound, above them in the dusk sky, and they both looked up. It was a great bird circling over them, wings wide, head cocked to peer down at the balcony.

"An eagle!" Bill shouted. "Heather! Quick! Come see!"

He ran inside to find the infra-red camera, bought especially and at great expense for nature shots. Heather came running out. She and Tommy stood and watched the eagle as it circled twice and swooped low over the apartment block. Heather clapped her hands in delight. Tommy called to it. It came almost close enough for the wind from its wing-beat to touch their faces.

Then it was gone.

Bill emerged from the apartment on to the balcony again, his camera loaded and ready, but there was no sign of their night visitor.

"Damn!" he said. Then smiled. "Ah well, plenty more eagles in the rainforest."

"It was watching us," Tommy said dramatically.

"Sure it was, " Bill said. "Come on, now. Supper time, and a good night's sleep."

It took a week to settle in, to begin to feel that Belore was their city, and that the small apartment was their home. Bill spent a day out at the site of the new dam, and Jean made contact—at last—with the organization for which she would be working. The rest of the time was their own and they made the most of it. For Tommy and Heather, though, the prospect of school loomed close. And a day before that dreaded event the Markham family went out to the edge of the world.

To picnic.

The site of the dam was at one of the wider curves of the Yuruan River. The land here had been denuded in a circle one mile wide around the critical construction point. The ground was hilly and the redness of the topsoil made it seem stark and arid. The encircling swathe of the emerald forest seemed to be silently watching and waiting its chance to creep back across the wilderness.

To arrive at the site, along the wide red track, was to emerge suddenly from a tunnel of green into an expanse of waste land, where hot dust formed a permanent orange cloud in the air above the great clearing. And the air was almost alive with sound, the vibrations of generators, chainsaws, bulldozers, earth-scoopers and the sirens calling shifts from one phase of clearing to another phase of digging.

The place was a confusion of activity. Great lumbering machines, painted yellow and with the AmazCo logo emblazoned on their sides, moved along the crudely marked tracks, or chewed and clawed at the earth, digging pits for the foundations of the buildings that would soon be erected here. So far, the site was a Portakabin City. Dust-smothered cars clustered by each small, bare hut. Men in hard-hats and shirtsleeves swarmed about the area, the sound of their voices lost against the roar of the machines.

"You'll go mad working here!" Jean shouted at Bill. He couldn't hear her. He braked sharply as a forty-ton earth-scoop suddenly trundled in front of the car. Tommy watched the immense machine in awe.

They parked the car. Standing in the heat and the noise, Bill checked in at the engineer's hut. Two Brazilian men appeared with him and shook hands with Jean, then the children. Jean thought that Bill introduced one of them as Enrico Costa, his immediate supervisor, but she couldn't be sure. The man smiled and Jean smiled; they spoke and the words were suffocated by the sudden raucous scream of a chainsaw a few meters away.

The air suddenly pulsed, a shock wave that made Tommy jump; a split second later the growling thunder of an explosion made them all turn towards the nearest tree line.

Four huge trees were slowly toppling out into the cleared land. The tallest must have been two hundred feet or more. The entire Markham family could not have held hands round its trunk.

"A Grandfather tree!" Bill shouted in Jean's ear. "Bulldozers can't shift them. Once they go, a thousand square meters of forest can be cleared in ten minutes."

Jean, Tommy and Heather watched the majestic death of the great plants. The tallest hovered, at an angle, while the others crashed down. Then it too inclined more steeply and kissed the dry earth with a great explosion of red dust. A dozen men moved in towards it and slung chains round its bulk. Two bulldozers roared and shuddered as they took the strain, then backed away from the jungle, towing the leviathan with them, towards the timber yard.

Behind them, other machines with scooped jaws began to strip the top few feet of forest from which the four trees had been blasted. The earth, the ferns and the underwood—all were removed with the ease of skin being drawn from a rabbit.

Heather blocked her ears against the noise and went back to the car. Tommy—being Tommy—*had* to have a ride in a bulldozer. Bill swung him up into the cab where the tolerant mestizo driver let the boy take the controls on a tight fifty-foot circle turn. Tommy was delighted. His blue eyes sparkled as his father helped him down. There was a fine coloring of red dust in the boy's blond hair.

"Come on, Tommy. Let's go see the jungle!" Bill shouted. Jean had taken the picnic hamper from the car. Bill grabbed the groundmat and his shotgun and the four of them walked away from the noisy center of operations, towards a part of the forest wall where there was no activity.

The land rose slightly towards the tree line. The air became clearer, cleaner, though just as hot. The noise from the works abruptly faded away. The engines and the continual chainsaws were suddenly very distant. It was a welcome and magic peace.

Now at last they could hear the sounds of the forest. The wall of vegetation was almost geometrically straight, sheered off by the machines that could eat such woodland in seconds. The edge, then, showed them scarred trees and a bulging confusion of green and red color from the undergrowth. Here, a bush chopped cleanly through, its red berries like drops of blood against the green. There, a sprawl of bristling roots, like grey spider's legs, flat upon the ground as they slowly began to reach back into the earth.

Smells, and a strange heat, exuded from the forest. The trees rustled and whispered. Out of sight, in the gloom, there was the occasional crack and creak of dry timber.

To step into this forest, as they did, was to enter a realm of scented twilight, but a twilight broken by the sharp-edged shafts of the sun as it gleamed through breaks in the fibrillating foliage. The smells were of flowers, and moss, and earth in its damp, living form. To turn from this dim, humid green to the baking, blasted red of the cleared land was to gaze from a primeval form of paradise into the reckless, blasted realm of hell. There was a comfort and a security in the crowded forest, the gentle touch of fronds, and webs, and the catch and snag of thorns—they seemed scary when regarded from outside, but became reassuring from inside, as if the forest tried to hold the family in its gentle grip, letting them see the barrenness beneath the skin, and the awful devastation that was progress.

Urging them to stay, but urging too softly, because Bill Markham was a man of progress, and of opportunity, and the jungle—to him—had a value measurable only in terms of its beauty, and its wildness; it was a zoo thing to him, a TV nature trail for real. He had no judgment or perception of this forest, beyond its association with the images that were created by technology, on the screen, in the color magazines that were read and discarded—nature's beauty, nature's plea, printed upon nature's pulped remains.

When Jean Markham looked across the void created by her people's ingenuity, she could not help seeing the forest as it had so recently been. Where they had walked, where the crumbled soil still showed their tracks, just days ago there had been a million years of undisturbed, moist growth, a place so remote and so ancient that when it had died, the entire world had died a little.

There, where the red dust drifted, was a place that had *always* been below the trees. It was strange, to her, to think of a place that had never seen the full light of the sun. A place of shade. And now that forest was just an imagined painting, a ghostly realm, pulped and sawn, and floating down the river.

When her husband stared at that same barren land, with the river curling so remotely through its center, he saw only the great rise of the AmazCo dam as it soon would be; and the town that would be built around it; and the roads, and the pylons, and the sheer concrete wall, against which even the huge earth-scoopers would seem mere toys. And he saw how that wall of sand and mortar would control the greatest of nature's forces, the inexorable surge and flow of water; he saw too, as a series of glittering city images, the way that power would be transformed into a utilitarian energy that would feed the hungry, restless future.

And yet there was no beauty, to Bill Markham, in images of the dam itself. There was beauty in the lines of stress, in the shape, in the strength of the wall, in the way it would dissipate all of nature's fury, making of evolution and geology a dead thing, a past thing, because the dam could hold against *anything*. It was the impenetrable barrier that would stop the unstoppable—only when it wished would water come through, towards the sea.

For twenty minutes they explored the forest's edge. Heather gathered leaves, fungi and flowers. Most of them ended up in the pocket of Jean's skirt. Tommy kept wandering a little too deeply into the jungle for his parent's liking, and Bill had to warn him quite severely about going out of earshot.

"There's an animal in there," Tommy said. Bill had already seen a snake, a small rodent and an evil-looking spider, but he thought it prudent not to tell the kids. Heather in particular, since the girl would have started poking around in the undergrowth looking for them.

"Probably a macaw," he said to the boy. "Either that or a howler . . ."

"A howler?"

"A type of monkey. Sits high up in the trees and drops certain things on passersby below."

"What things?"

"Figure it out for yourself. Howler monkeys made life hell for the *conquistadores* a few hundred years ago." He grinned at his son. "A constant rainstorm."

"You mean they *peed*!" Tommy burst into laughter as he remembered the TV program on the Spanish destruction of the Incas. He also remembered the time at Red Park Zoo when Heather had advanced a little too near to some primate—another sort of monkey—as it had spreadeagled itself on the cage bars. The animal's greeting had been hot, wet and impressively accurate. Heather—drenched—had thought it was hilarious.

At the very edge of the forest a machine-scarred Grandfather tree still stood, its roots half-exposed, its life measurable, now, in hours. From one of its high branches hung strands of liana, the fibrous vine-like growth that parasitized most tropical trees. Bill—remembering the liana swings of his own childhood—tested one of the thicker strands until he was satisfied that it would take Tommy's weight.

Heather first, then Tommy, swung on the liana, pushed through a wide arc as they screamed and laughed, twenty yards out into the sun, twenty yards into the jungle: Heather burned her hands a little, although she didn't complain. Tommy just wanted more. It was an *exhilarating* feeling.

"Push me more. Push me *more*!" he cried.

And Bill reached high to his dangling, flying form, propelling it back into the moist undergrowth, waiting for the delighted figure to come hurtling through the leaves again, out into the sun . . .

He knew exactly what Tommy was experiencing, the exhilarating contrast between the bright heat and the warm shade, the sense of space and the sudden plunging into gloomy confinement. Swinging between two worlds.

3

Jean had spread out the large picnic blanket and was carefully placing the plates and mugs round its edges. There were no insects. It was as if all living things had been stripped from the land, and nothing came further than the forest edge, too frightened that it would be consumed by the waste land.

The red soil blew slightly, the first dust already forming on the parched skin of the earth. Jean tried to keep it from the food, but as Bill and Tommy skidded down on the ground to eat, a small storm of dry grit drifted over the picnic area.

Bill buttered bread and mixed the salad. Heather tried to cut the sandwiches and somehow managed to get a thick layer of peanut butter all over her hands. Tommy poked in the soil with a stick.

An ant appeared from the hole he had made and scurried away across the woollen table-cloth landscape, veering between the steel girders of forks and the monolithic china towers that were the dishes. Heather was delighted. She reached over and picked up the insect in one sticky fist, ignoring her father's sudden stern look.

"I *like* ants."

"I don't," Tommy said.

"Put it down, sweetheart. They can give a nasty bite."

Heather looked crestfallen. "Ants can love people too!"

"Sure, honey. Put it down, now."

The ant, liberated by paternal decree, began its next nightmare journey, lost against the dry earth. Directionless, it would know home when it found it.

They ate cold chicken and peanut butter sandwiches. Bill decided to reinforce the basic lessons of the new country.

"What's the first law of nature?"

Tommy said, "Nothing is what it seems."

"Ten out of ten," said Jean. She leaned towards him and pointed at his chest. "You have permission to lick the peanut butter off your shirt."

With his mouth full of chicken, Bill Markham went on, "What's the second law? Come on, you kids. You've shirked language and geography, but you'd better not shirk *survival*."

Heather said, "Don't poke snakes with sticks."

"Absolutely. Avoid 'em at all costs."

With a little frown of anxiety, the girl added, "Not even the *small* ones? I *like* the small ones."

"I don't," Tommy said.

"Not even the small ones, honey. Small bite, big trouble. Come on. What else?"

Tommy said, "Don't poke dead animals."

"Right! The possum posture!" Bill leaned towards the children. "Did I ever tell you about the Awful Anteater? I did? Then it's worth telling again . . ."

The tale of the Awful Anteater had now become funny simply because of Bill Markham's insistence on repeating it at every possible opportunity, despite the loud cries of anguish and protest from the rest of the family. But it was a true story, and had not been funny at the time.

He had been to South America many times, but the first time

had been as a child of about his own son's age. He had come to Venezuela with his father, and they had stayed in a large house, with lush gardens to the rear and a ragged tarmac road to the front.

The anteater had walked across the lawn while the Spanish gardener had been pruning the roses. The gardener's main tool was a machete, always carried at his hip. A useful garden instrument, but of course a valuable weapon.

When an animal comes blindly out of the forest it usually means trouble; the animal might be diseased, or wounded, or just mad in one of several animal madness ways. You can run, or you can kill. An anteater looks harmless, but it can easily kill a child if maddened.

The gardener knew no better. He struck the beast three times with his machete, killing it, he was sure. He dragged the carcass to the compost and left it there.

A few hours later the anteater's body was on the lawn again, sixty yards from the rubbish tip. The gardener saw it and imagined that either a dog had dragged it there, or it had crawled there on its own, not dead only wounded.

It had been crawling directly towards the house.

The gardener prodded it with his machete. And for good measure he struck it again across the skull, breaking the bone.

And then he turned his back.

In a second the animal, which was in pain and enraged and had been simulating death, had clawed him open. An anteater digs in the ground, and its claws are like sharpened steel. No higher than the gardener's thighs, it ripped the man's legs open. Neither beast nor man survived the day.

Bill Markham repeated the lesson to be learned from that horrific incident in his own childhood. "You must *never* turn your back. Never assume that because something is pretty it's safe. Look at Heather, for example. She's quite the most deadly thing in the family." They all laughed. "And like the forest . . . it seems so peaceful, doesn't it? So quiet, so warm. But you must *always* be wary."

"Can't we even play with the spiders?" Heather asked plaintively. "Just the *little* ones?"

"Especially not the spiders," Bill said, exchanging a look of despair with Jean.

Tommy stared at his sister. After a moment he muttered, "For a girl you're real *weird*."

"Not weird to want pets," Heather said gloomily.

4

When they had finished eating, Bill leaned back on his elbows and Jean came round to sit quietly with him. They stared down the slope of land to the distant activity round the gleaming river. Tommy and Heather walked back to the great wall of vegetation and began to pursue their own explorations at the jungle's edge.

"Stay where we can see you, okay?" Jean called. As Bill tugged the shotgun closer she asked him, "Are there jaguars this close to the edge?"

"I don't think so. The explosions frighten them off. I'm more worried about Heather touching insects."

But the kids just walked along the cut forest edge, picking up leaves, bits of twig, and swinging on lianas as much as their small strength could manage.

Jean Markham said, "When it's built it's really going to be something. The dam, I mean. How much more forest is to be cleared?"

"Not a great deal, now. A few thousand acres where they'll make the landing strip and community center. The logging companies will move in, though. The whole area will be grassland and farms in a few years."

"Seems a shame. The jungle's so beautiful . . ."

Bill Markham smiled thinly. "As Costa always says, there's a hell of a lot of jungle."

"And a hell of a lot of people cutting it down from the edge. The Indians are getting squeezed out."

Bill grunted, the only comment he felt able to make at the moment. He was still confused about the forest, and its indigenous population. Costa had already referred to him as "our young American liberal." It was quite clear that few, if any, of the engineers and builders working on the dam had given any real thought to the growing, and frightening, degree to which the rainforest was being cleared. Costa always said, "There's a hell of a lot of forest. You leave it a year and it grows back over miles. The forest can look after itself."

"And the Indians?" Bill had asked.

"There are only two types of Indians, my liberal friend," Costa had said slowly and pointedly. "Those that live under Brazilian supervision, and those who come *out* of the forest to live under Brazilian supervision."

"What about the Indians that stay hidden?"

"There *are* no Indians that stay hidden," Costa had said sharply.

"But that's just not true. I heard that there was evidence for at least four family groups, uncontacted by the outside."

Costa had just stared at him, a look that combined irritation with pity. Then he smiled. "There are no such Indians." He stepped a little closer. "I heard you're a fine engineer, Bill. My advice to you is that you do your job, then go home. To stay too long in Brazil might well break your heart . . ."

With a guilty glance towards his parents, who were stretched out on the rug staring wistfully into the far distance, Tommy scrambled up over the earthy root of a tall tree and crawled into the damp of the forest. Where he had entered was rather like a cavernous and exuberant tangle of trunks, branches and the rope-like strands of liana. Some of the wood he touched just crumbled in his hands. The underfoot was soft and rotten. Sunlight gleamed sporadically through the dense overhead foliage, and in its occasional rays he saw bright colors, and unnerving, rapid movements.

Close by, a bird trilled; a short, unfamiliar song. It was answered from deeper in the jungle. His body began to shiver. He jerked back as a wet leaf, the size of his head, gently touched his cheek. A sudden shaft of sunlight illuminated a dark plant, its smooth features streaked with white. It looked uncannily like a human face, its eyes closed.

Again the bird song. Again the answer, closer now. Again the sense of stealthy movement through the dense undergrowth.

Tommy turned back towards the dimly perceivable outside, the place where the light was strongest. He felt unnerved now. He felt that he was being watched, and it frightened him slightly. This was an altogether darker and more oppressive part of the jungle than the glade where they had played a few minutes before.

As he stepped back towards the day he stopped and his heart missed a beat. A snake was suspended in the air before him, just a foot away. It was horizontal, and quite motionless, blocking his path . . .

And then he realized that it wasn't a snake at all. It was an arm, a human arm. The snake's head blossomed into fingers, and the fingers came towards him and gently touched his dank, blond hair. He looked up and above the arm was a face, watching him. The face was black and white, with a pattern of red diamonds on the cheeks. The eyes were bright in the thin sunlight. The skin was wrinkled. An old man.

As Tommy watched him, so the old man smiled, then whistled quickly: the sound of the bird.

Tommy's shadow, falling suddenly over Bill Markham, made the man jump. He looked up at his son, from where he lay on the rug, burning in the heat, then frowned as he saw the way the boy was shaking. Jean noticed too. "What's happened, Tommy?"

"There're people in there," Tommy said plaintively, and his big eyes looked from one to the other of the adults. "They scared me."

Bill reached for his shotgun and glanced quickly at Jean. Then he said to Tommy, "What sort of people?"

"Smiling people . . ."

The expression meant nothing to Bill, and it certainly didn't sound frightening. What had Tommy seen? Shadows? Or maybe one of the workers, walking in the forest, playing tricks on the kids. Or perhaps it was just Tommy's imagination. He was desperate to see "real" Indians, so he was starting to imagine them.

Bill stood up, checked the shotgun carefully, then—with his hand on his son's shoulder—walked back up to the tree line. He clambered up the rough ground, then pulled Tommy up after him. They were in the bright area of the forest's edge, but Tommy walked cautiously towards the gloom a few yards away.

"Where were they?" Bill asked.

"Through there . . ."

They pushed through the lush undergrowth. Bill used the shotgun to push aside the strands of vine and creeper. He parted the broad leaves and peered carefully into the musty spaces so revealed.

He saw nothing.

Tommy walked close behind him, clutching at the belt of his jeans.

"Can't see anything, son . . ."

"They were here. They were smiling at me."

"They don't sound too hostile," Bill said. A few yards away, deeper in the forest, a bird called—a brief, shrill sound in the heavy silence.

Tommy immediately jumped, his eyes widening. Bill noticed this and grinned. "That's just a damned parrot . . ."

"That's *them*!"

"It's a bird, Tommy. Birds live in trees, remember? There's nothing here. There's nothing to be worried about . . ."

He broke the breech of his shotgun, ruffled Tommy's hair, and then led the way back to the open land. "Time to go, kids," he said. Heather had scrambled up after the two men and stood staring into the darker confines of the jungle. Bill took her hand and led her back through the root tangle where the machines had cut the land away.

"Come on, Tommy!"

"Coming . . ."

Tommy followed slowly. The bird sang again and he turned to look towards it. There was a movement above him, in the dense foliage. He looked up but there was just the green leaves, and sunlight, and the wire-like strands of liana. Next to him there was a bush. He reached out to the bush and tugged at the leaves, shaking it, rustling it . . . then he parted the leaves and peered at what he could see there.

It startled him slightly, but he was puzzled and intrigued, now. He peered more closely at the mask. It was shaped like a human face. The hair on the mask was dyed red. The cheeks were decorated with circular white patterns. The lips were outlined with blue. The eyes were closed, the lids spotted with green.

As he stared at the mask, the eyes of the mask opened. The lips parted and whispered something to him. They whispered his name . . .

"Tom . . . Ma . . ."

From outside the forest, Bill's voice called sharply. "Tommy! Come on. We're going home, now!"

Tommy began to walk towards the bright daylight.

"Tom . . . Ma . . ." the mask whispered, and Tommy hesitated . . .

Turned back . . .

Jean had almost finished packing up the picnic things. As Bill approached she glanced up. "Did you find anything?"

"Imagination. Bird song. Shadows. That's all. Indians don't come this close to the edge."

"Where's Tommy?"

"He's right here . . ."

Bill turned, then froze. Heather was swinging on the liana up by the jungle's edge. Tommy was nowhere to be seen. And yet . . . And yet Bill could have sworn that the boy had come running out of the forest and followed him down, back to the picnic site.

He turned back to Jean, who was slowly straightening up, the plastic mugs in her hand. She was staring at him. And Bill Markham suddenly realized that the two of them were exchanging a gaze of growing terror. He frowned. His heart started to pump with noisy energy. The bare land, and the forest, began to swim in his vision.

Jean stepped towards him, the mugs falling from her grasp. All the blood had drained from her face . . .

In that instant they were aware of it, sensing the danger, sensing the tragedy. They moved towards each other, but the daylight had slipped away, the sun dimmed, the warmth drained away into a terrible chill.

"Tommy . . ." Bill said. "Oh my God . . ."

And then they were running. Bill grabbed the shotgun. Jean screamed the boy's name. Heather started to cry as she saw the panic and terror in her parents' faces. They flung themselves into the bush, scrabbling and crawling into the gloom.

"Tommy! *Tommy*! Answer me!"

"Oh *God*! What can have happened?"

"*Tommy*!"

They were two wild figures, flailing through the undergrowth, plunging recklessly through thorns and the saturated clusters of silk grass, brushing aside the trailing lianas, weaving their way between the dark trunks of trees.

Around them, bird and animal life fled. They heard a bird sing, deep in the forest, the same bird song that had sounded when Tommy had said, "That's them."

Jean was sobbing. Her voice became almost hysterically high as she called for her son. Bill shouted too, and his throat grazed. He realized, with a sudden, sickening wave of despair, that it was too late. He discharged both barrels of the shotgun up into the air, then reloaded and raced back towards the edge.

As he ran something caught his eye. Behind him, Jean was still frantically screaming into the darkness, her body like that of a wild cat, crashing through the plant life, breaking through screen after endless screen of the jungle.

What Bill had seen was a pair of black and white feathers. As he drew close he saw that the feathers were attached to a long, elegantly shafted arrow, stuck horizontally into a tree. He wrenched the arrow out and inspected the narrow stone blade. He managed to break the thin shaft during this violent motion, and he cursed loudly.

Then he went to the edge of this emerald world and fired twice again. Already, a stream of men and four bulldozers—alerted by the first shots—were racing towards them.

At dusk, the last of the searchers emerged from the dense forest, brushing off the dampness and the pollen that invariably coated the clothing at this time of the evening. They shook their heads, or shrugged, and one of them spoke sad words in Portuguese. Two of the last of the searchers were shirt Indians, only two years estranged from the forest world that had been the home of their ancestors for thousands more. One of them spoke to Enrico Costa, pointed to the wood, made two or three elaborate gestures with his hands, then walked away. Costa nodded, then came over to where Bill and Jean Markham were standing, a forlorn and bedraggled pair, their arms around each other.

Costa said, "I am so sorry. This is a terrible welcome to Brazil for you."

"What have you found?" Bill asked hoarsely.

"Tracks. The Indians must have been watching you for some time. But the tracks end about one hundred paces into the forest. I am very sorry."

"Definitely Indians, then," Jean said, "and not a wild animal."

Costa nodded sympathetically. When Jean turned to Bill and said, "So there's hope. They might bring him back," he squeezed her tightly and glanced at the Brazilian, who almost imperceptibly shook his head.

"I'll find him, Jean," Bill whispered, drawing her even closer. "I swear to God I'll find him."

There were tears in her eyes as she looked up. "*We'll* find him. We'll find him together." She was shaking violently, only just in control. "We've got to . . . nothing is more important, nothing—not the dam, not us—nothing. Nothing but Tommy . . . we've *got* to find him, Bill. Now. We've got to start *now* . . ."

Behind them the engines of the bulldozers roared into life, as machines and men began the slow journey back to the base camp below.

PART TWO

Journey into the World

1

From his spacious office in the cabin-city that stretched out from the dam, Bill Markham heard the sound of the helicopter that had come to fetch him back to Belore. He hadn't quite finished tidying up his desk. He still had to pack away the plans for the pump-housings which were now almost the last structures that remained to be built.

He decided to leave the mess—Harry Margolis would tidy up for him tomorrow—and he grabbed up his pack, then checked around the office. The photograph of Tommy, on the wall above his desk, was curling slightly at the edges. On a last impulse he plucked the picture down and tucked it into his inside pocket.

In the ten years that had passed since the Smiling People had stolen his son, Bill Markham had changed very little. There was no grey in his hair, no sagging of his features, no noticeable change at all in the man who had gone from thirty to forty years of age in a country that remained alien to him, with a family that had never recovered from the tragedy of the abduction. No change, that is, except in his eyes. He had always been a solemn man, and his eyes had always gleamed with good humor, giving a hint of the reckless, trickster youth that remained behind the mask of the mature man.

Gone now. All humor vanished. His eyes were dead. When they were not dead they were angry. He had long since ceased to show sadness.

The helicopter had landed on the flat landing strip at the base of the sloping rise of the huge dam. Markham ran quickly towards it, tugging at his anorak. It was a surprisingly cool day and had been raining constantly—though not heavily—for hours. The whole site was drab and uninviting, an expanse of concrete, clustered shacks, the quarries formed by strip-mining where the jungle had been cleared, and of course the imposing rise of the barrier itself.

As the helicopter rose abruptly into the air, Markham again experienced a sensation of awe as the sheer wall of grey-yellow slipped endlessly by. A great curved curtain of smooth rock, the construction dwarfed the cars that ferried men along its top.

The helicopter turned east, passed over the dam and along the broad ribbon of the river. The valley, here, was still forested, although a strip a hundred yards wide had been cleared on each side of the river itself. Skimming low over the tree tops, as the pilot flew a course directly towards the distant city, Markham saw again the thin curls of smoke that rose from hidden camps below. It was always the same, at this time of year. From the top of the dam itself the silent presence in the forest could easily be observed, and he had often stood there and watched. He had counted ten fires, last year. All close to the forest edge, all on the deep jungle side.

But the teams who went to investigate could never find so much as an ash pile.

The fire makers were an invisible people. This place may have been a place of pilgrimage for them for centuries. They hid in the jungle and watched the dam, and slipped away into the greenery whenever the outsiders came to investigate.

The streamers of smoke were soon lost from sight, and Markham stared silently at the wilderness below, thinking about the trek he was about to undertake, his tenth journey deep into the rainforest. Only when the distant skyline began to resolve into the towers and blocks of Belore did he turn his mind to the "problem" that Landsat, watching the Amazon from twenty thousand miles up, had begun to detect.

2

Markham disliked the AmazCo Belore offices with a vengeance. He spent as little time in them as possible. After the noise and open sky of the dam site, he found the muffled, partitioned rooms and the cool ionized air of the office block an environment that could rapidly induce strong feelings of claustrophobia in him. In the ten years he had worked for AmazCo he had managed to acquire an office suite with a balcony and a view over the distant rainforest. But he was always restless when he worked in Belore, and inevitably the work, and his mood, suffered.

Enrico Costa met him at the roof landing pad and led him briskly down through the warren of corridors to the main display room. The little man seemed nervous, but was clearly relieved to see Markham.

"What exactly did Landsat show up?"

"Flood transfer," Costa said, pushing through double glass doors. "Perrera is on the edge . . ."

"He's always on the edge."

"This time it's bad. Accusations of miscalculation." Costa glanced cautiously at the American before continuing. "Faulty design . . ."

Markham allowed the merest hint of a smile to touch his lips. In ten years his design engineering had come under fire many times. He was used to it, although he had never before been so summarily dragged back from the site.

"That was my fault," Costa confessed. Ahead of them was a big open-plan room, its wall space covered with computer screens and display units. Joseph Perrera and two other dark-suited men stood talking in the center of the room. Costa went on quickly, "He's talking about postponing your leave."

"No way," Markham said firmly. "I go tomorrow. It's all set."

"That's why I thought: get you back quick. Get it sorted out."

"Get what sorted out?"

Costa said grimly, "They don't think the dam will hold."

The two strangers—AmazCo executives—shook hands with Markham, but Perrera's greeting was short and sour. The Project Supervisor was a continual irritation to Bill Markham. The man panicked at the least hint of delay, or the least sign of difficulty, even though he achieved wonders of co-operation between different aspects of the work and different sections of the workforce. He was a short, stocky man with smooth, ruddy features and a mouth that looked anatomically incapable of smiling.

He led the way quickly to the Landsat-link screen, and Enrico Costa sat down and punched up the last satellite image of the Amazon basin. He enhanced the color, then brought up the detail, enlarging the familiar bend in the Yuruan River until the dam itself could be seen. He scrolled north and west, up-river from the dam, then brought the image up under even higher magnification. Markham watched the screen. He could see that Costa was focusing in on a D S W, a Dual System Weakness. The two winding streams that he could see came within a few yards of each other, separated by a wooded ridge. The streams were each part of a different river system, the Yuruan and most likely the Pirikatu. Each of those rivers, though, was just one of the many hundreds of tributaries of the vast Amazon itself. The Amazon's drainage basin was immense, a great network of water routes fanning out through the millions of square miles of rainforest.

"A D S W," Costa said, tapping the screen with his finger. Perrera shuffled and sighed impatiently, actions designed to urge Enrico Costa to brief Markham more quickly. "There are two hundred and nine such weaknesses up-river of the AmazCo dam."

"Two hundred and ten," Markham corrected.

Costa shook his head. He moved the image a fraction west. Markham leaned closer and saw where the ridge between the streams was now crossed by a thin silver glitter. Water. "That happened at 6 a.m. yesterday, after a storm in the Arucur area. The flood jumped the ridge and the Pirikatu system fed into our own Yuruan for about twenty minutes. That's standing water on the ridge top, but the ridge has been cut through. The level in the Pirikatu system has dropped, but that jump should not have happened. It made us look at the whole river system." Costa glanced up, his face anxious. Markham remained calm, trying to grasp fully the point to which Costa was building.

Perrera said, "The point *is*, Bill, the level is in the normal flood range. But the river isn't *in* flood. If it *does* flood—say an extended and very heavy rainstorm—we calculate that water will jump across half the weak points."

"Jesus," Markham said softly. But he kept outwardly impassive, giving no sign of the sudden shock that had stopped his heart for a moment or two. "What's pushed the level up?"

"That's a good question," Costa said, swinging slightly in his chair. "One possibility is a drop in the fixed water level in the forest. It's something the conservationists have been nagging about for years. As the forest shrinks it changes its nature slightly. A 1 per cent drop in the amount of water fixed in the jungle puts a hell of a lot of water into the drainage network."

"It's more likely," Joseph Perrera said stiffly, "that there's a silt build-up down-stream. Erosion waste from where the river has been cleared too clumsily. Or maybe dumping from the building works—places like Emmakka, strip-mining—using the river like a sewer. It's been going on for twenty years. A change in down-river topography could put back pressure into the drainage network. River level rises. It's been happening so slowly that we hadn't noticed it."

Costa turned back to the screen. "We calculate that between ten and twenty miles of water would be added to the Yuruan system *per stream* if the jump-over happens!"

"That's a lot of water," Markham murmured.

"You're damn right that's a lot of water," Perrera said irritably. "Which is why you're here. How about the dam? What expectation of this was programmed into your design?"

Markham stared at the man coldly. "Let's work it out, shall we?"

He felt less confident than he looked or sounded. Costa knew this, of course, but Enrico Costa took courage from the young engineer's cool. Markham sat down at a computer screen and played with numbers.

His heart was beating fast. The dam was huge, many years in the building, but in Markham's mind it was just a series of stress points, weak points, strong points and redundancies. He could imagine a wall of water striking it and rolling back. He could also imagine the wall of water that would strike the dam and destroy it. Force and counterforce. The equation had a great deal of flexibility, but the sides of it would have to balance at a certain critical point.

He went for the worst scenario imaginable. An extended rainstorm that caused a water jump at every one of the two hundred and nine weak points between tributary systems. That would put four thousand miles of Pirikatu water into the Yuruan River, but it would be spread over eighteen hundred miles. That, nevertheless, would mean a wave front riding on top of the flood swell, and the wave front would be traveling fast, and could reach half the height of the dam. But there would be valley-side drag; the water would crawl up the hills lowering the central flow.

Markham ignored all the favorable aspects of the equation. He came up with an impact force and stared at the calculation carefully. It was dauntingly close to being critical. Unnervingly close to being unstoppable. But Perrera wouldn't know that.

He said, "It'll hold. My dam will hold. And that's under the worst imaginable flood."

Perrera looked sour, even though the other three men had all exhaled noisily with relief, and Costa had even applauded.

"Your dam, Bill?"

With the merest smile of acknowledgment to the Brazilian, Markham corrected himself. "Our dam." He slapped Costa on the shoulder. "Good try, Enrico. You had me worried there."

Costa grinned. "I had me worried too. What about splash-over? Will there be much splash-over?"

"Of course there will. If you see the flood coming, you get everyone and everything out of the dam area, and fast."

As they walked to the exit door, Perrera suddenly extended his hand to Bill Markham. "I have something to check out. Well done, Bill."

Markham shook hands awkwardly, smiling coolly. "The dam'll hold."

"You're off on vacation, then. Six weeks up-river."

"That's right."

"Well . . . the break will be good for you. I shan't say enjoy yourself. I'll just wish you . . . I'll wish you luck. Good luck, Bill."

"Thanks."

Enrico Costa walked with Markham, down to the building's main entrance. "May you and your family be holidaying in Europe next year," Costa said, and smiled. "In other words: good luck."

"Thanks, Rico."

"Take care, Bill. Don't turn your back . . ."

Markham laughed. "I shan't. See you in six weeks."

3

When Bill drove up to the gates of the San Verona orphanage and waved to her, Jean Markham was only halfway down the line of sixty children waiting for their measles shots. She straightened up and waved back, then gestured that she still had an hour's work to do. Bill—dressed in his trekking fatigues—signaled back that he would wait. He blew her a kiss. She blew one back. In the passenger seat of the Markhams' weather-worn Range Rover, the saturnine features of the anthropologist, Uwe Werner, twisted into a grimace of acknowledgement. Jean, who detested the German, ignored him.

The line of ragged children shuffled forward, bringing one or two more into the shade of the mango tree beneath which the medical bench had been set up, and sending one or two more back to the crowded lawns of the old colonial house that was now the orphanage. There, in bemused silence, they would wait for food, and clothing, and later for the walk indoors to a rough wool hammock.

The sixty children who were being immunized had arrived that morning from the overflowing Rescue Center at Maenosa. Some were quite old—aged ten or eleven, although none ever knew exactly—but most were just five or six. Their drawn faces and spindly limbs made them seem pathetic, large eyes pleading for attention. Most of them were half-Indian, cast out by families or communities. The mix in their blood was usually European, but there were a handful of children with Negroid features, and an even smaller number with a bizarre Japanese look about them. Those few children were irresistibly attractive, but tended to be the shyest, and most uncooperative.

Jean smiled and spoke to each child who shuffled past. She fingered arms that were more bone than flesh, and pushed the tiny needle into anything that felt like muscle. Some of the children were so emaciated that they were channeled away from the main throng. Others had clear signs of malaria, or tuberculosis, and these were whisked into the tall, ramshackle old building, where there was a small and overcrowded hospital ward.

In the five years that she had worked at this orphanage Jean had taken nursing qualifications, and was now contemplating a medical degree. The thing that was stopping her from taking that logical step was the thought of three years away from the field. The children were a part of her life now, and she a part of theirs. She was well aware of the degree of "compensation" that had been involved in her growing passion for helping the orphans, but it remained an unspoken knowledge. Unspoken, that is, save by the insufferable Uwe Werner. She had never forgiven the man for his blunt and callous comment to her, three years ago.

"When one can do so little, Mrs. Markham, perhaps it is better to do nothing. But I admire you. You look after other people's lost children, and maybe someone somewhere is looking after your own lost boy . . ."

But Werner was now an integral part of the exploration team. His advice and knowledge of the forest Indians had been of immense help in the early years of their search for Tommy. When Jean had finally decided not to go on the six-week treks anymore, Werner had taken her place. He worked in Venezuela, but now matched his leave with the Markhams' and turned up, never late, ready for the long and hazardous journey into the heart of the jungle.

Jean, for her part, did not miss those terrible weeks of searching the swamps, and the rivers, and the steaming, hot gloom. She missed the hope that always accompanied the first week or so. And she missed the closeness that she and Bill always came to feel in the middle days. But she did not miss the agonizing disappointment of the closing weeks, when they would have to begin the long trek back.

Because that loneliness, and the pain, had been a burden shared they had managed to keep their determination strong. Other couples—from the start questing individually, apart from each other—might have abandoned hope long before.

After ten years, both Bill and Jean Markham simply *knew* that Tommy was still alive. And that they *would* find him. And that they would be a family again. Tommy was not dead, and he was not lost to them forever. This belief was the pivot around which the Markhams' lives revolved.

So every year, for six weeks, Bill and Uwe Werner went inwards, trying to find the hidden tribes, asking, endlessly asking, about the Smiling People who used a single pair of black and white feathers on their arrows; and Jean drove the forest edge, contacting missions, logging camps, Indian reservations, watching and listening for a word, or a hint, that an unknown tribe had been contacted . . . or a blond Indian boy had been seen.

The last of the refugees dutifully, if reluctantly, submitted herself to the needle, then grinned at Jean and said something in a language that could have been Portuguese, or might as easily have been Xingu. It was hard to tell since the child lisped appallingly, and in any case was missing two teeth. A tiny tot of about five, she seemed to become urgent, and Jean realized that she wasn't just *holding* her crude wooden doll, she was pushing it towards the woman in the white coat.

Again the words; again the plea. Jean grasped the meaning. The girl wanted the needle protection for her toy. With a smile, the woman dutifully pinched the wooden arm and jabbed it with a needle. As she held the doll she found herself staring at the angular face, with its roughly painted features. Its hair was made of feathers. Black feathers. Her unfocused thoughts were abruptly interrupted as the small child tugged back her doll, smiled broadly, and ran off to join the others, queuing up (with remarkable restraint) for food.

"That's it. I'm finished. And I'm off."

Her assistant, a middle-aged Brazilian man who helped out in all quarters of the orphanage and who seemed skilled at everything, including surgery, stopped her from doing any tidying up.

"I'll see to this. You go and have a nice holiday."

"Thanks, Tola." She gave the smiling man a hug and a kiss. "See you in four weeks."

4

The Markhams lived in the same apartment that had been theirs on their first arrival. Somehow there had never seemed the time to move to more luxurious and spacious accommodation. Somehow, the effort had always seemed too daunting. And besides—this was the only home in Brazil that Tommy had known (even though he had known it for a mere few days) and if he was to return to them, this would be the only place he would remember.

Not that he would recognize it. The Markhams' house had become nothing short of a museum. Almost every inch of wall was covered with some picture or artefact gathered during the nine long searches. There were war shields, headdresses, shrunken heads, spears and arrows, racks of feathered weapon-tips, masks and endless photographs and maps of the rainforest and its indigenous population.

The rainforest had been an obsessive and serious study for them all since Tommy had been taken, and each of the Markhams had specialized in certain areas. Heather, with her fascination for natural history, was the biology buff. She knew what to eat, where to find it, how to catch it, how to avoid poisoning. She taught everything she knew to her father. Heather was fifteen years old now, a bright and very attractive girl who was excelling at school and trying to decide between a career in medicine and one in natural history. She did not share that part of her parents' obsession which was based on grief and a desperation to reunite the family. When she spoke of Tommy she spoke of a strange amalgamation of the child that Tommy had been and the elder brother she still imagined. A man–boy who existed only in her own mind.

Jean's field of expertise was the anthropology of the forest people. She knew everything that was known about the tribal hunting-grounds, the movement of communities, the body patterning of different groups, and their relative "safety" in terms of outside contact. Cannibalism was not prevalent in the jungle, but it existed. So did curare, liberally smeared on arrow tips. Too many explorers and missionaries had been killed by a people they had never even known was watching them. It was the capricious nature of the forest, its dangerous ambiguity: a few miles could separate communities which differed totally in their attitudes to strangers.

All three in the family spoke a number of Indian languages, but Bill had made it a priority to become familiar with as many as possible. In fact, he spoke fifteen different indigenous tongues (excluding Portuguese) and could manage four or five dialects of each. He now knew more than a hundred different words for the breezes that blew through the forest, from the Kura-Wai *yakara*, which meant "young girl's breath," and described the gentle, almost imperceptible breeze that ruffled the undergrowth at the height of the day, to the Muru word *juwaka-wak*. Translated literally, *juwaka-wak* referred to the impressive flatulence of the "wild" pigs that the Muru kept. In forest terms it meant the early morning breeze that swept the forest as the upper air in the jungle environment heated up faster than the ground air, drawing with it all the rich, fetid smells of the litter.

In the Markham household the word had rapidly been applied to describe Bill's favourite beef and bean stew. Heather tended to stay with friends when *juwaka-wak* was on the menu for the evening.

On this first evening of the tenth six-week search, they ate quickly and simply, then cleared the table so that the detailed route map could be spread out. While Heather helped her father pack his rucksack—a by now much worn Lowe Alpine Systems Trekker—Jean sat with Uwe Werner and briefed the man on the preliminary route that Bill had chosen, and on the likely tribal encounters they would make.

Werner seemed tired. He was less provocative than Jean remembered him, and she felt slightly guilty at having snubbed him earlier. He looked older, too, although in appearance he remained somewhere between a hippy and a mercenary. Uwe Werner was very tall, very lean, and wore his greasy black hair down to his shoulders. Usually he tied his hair into a pigtail, but as he pored over the map of the Amazon he wore it loose, and kept sweeping it back across his forehead, holding it there while he studied the route. He had a single eyebrow, a thick band of dark hair that gashed across his brow from temple to temple. Heather referred to him as "the werewolf."

"This is a good plan," he said, stabbing a finger down on the new map. "It takes us close to some important Mission stations, and gives us a wide band of unknown forest to try. A very good plan."

Jean was pleased that there was none of the usual discussion and argument, opinions expressed for the sake of expressing them. She and Bill had considered the trip very carefully. It was designed to get the two men up-river very fast, and give them brief contact with about twenty Mission and "rescue" stations, the sort of outpost that was usually the first to make contact with unknown tribes, or hear of unusual encounters in the deep jungle. After that they had the whole of the area recently designated *makira aku* to explore, although they would only have time for a single trek through the vast expanse of rainforest that covered this hilly and unknown terrain.

Jean said, "There's evidence, now, for two or three groups living in the *makira aku* who have made no outside contact. They're known about by other Indian tribes, but as fast as an Indian settles outside the forest he seems to forget about the past."

"I've seen it happen," Werner said. "We must hope to make friendly contact at a Mission. One of the stations where the latex is brought, maybe. Half in this world, half in the next."

Jean went on, "What is especially appealing about the area is that it *can* be seen to connect with the site of the AmazCo dam. There's a natural sequence of ridges and shallow waterways between the two sites, and that's the sort of terrain that often makes for a 'hunt-trail.' "

Werner rubbed his jaw thoughtfully. "A hunt-trail of hundreds of miles. That's impressive."

"It's not common, but the more we learn about the different groups the more we are surprised by some of the aspects of their past lives."

"It's good," Werner repeated, sitting back in his chair and clasping his hands behind his head. "A good plan. And this time I have a feeling . . . we're going to find something!"

Jean smiled thinly. "You say that every year, Mr. Werner."

"This year is different. I have had dreams. Dreams of the forest. Dreams of a strange people with strange markings on their body. My dreams seem to be telling me that we shall be making contact with an unknown group. As an anthropologist this excites me greatly. Maybe they will be the ones who took Tommy."

Jean folded the map carefully. "I'm surprised that a man like you would put his faith in dreams." She had meant that Werner, as a scientist, would be expected to be more pragmatic. She realized, though, that her words had sounded sardonic. Before she could make amends, however, Werner had responded ironically, "From you, a person who lives a dream of hope, the criticism is unusual."

"The fact of our hope, Mr. Werner, is not a dream, it is a belief."

Heather had noisily thrown one of the equipment bags on to the sitting-room floor, an act that protested against Werner's sharp tongue. Bill was making soothing motions towards his daughter, and the German saw this, and smiled awkwardly. He reached out and gently touched Jean's arm. "I'm sorry. I meant no offense."

"I'm sure you didn't," Jean said, and took a deep breath, which she expired in a very welcome sigh. "I wish I was going with you."

"I should be glad of your company," Werner said. He stared at the woman, heavy eyebrows bunched as he assessed and contemplated her.

Jean said, "It always comes back to one thing. The not knowing. It's the not knowing that's so hard to live with. The uncertainty."

"I can understand that. I can understand that very well."

"There are times," Jean continued, "times when I feel panic. If we just *knew* . . . if we could just know for *sure* that Tommy was—"

She broke off suddenly—not liking the sound of her own voice, the weakness it displayed. She had been about to say that if they could have known for sure that Tommy was alive they might find more help, and a greater determination. But Uwe Werner misunderstood. Bluntly, he said, "If you could just be sure that he was dead then you could get on with your lives. You would be free, in a way. Yes, that I can comprehend too."

Jean felt her face flush with anger. Behind her both Heather and Bill were staring at Werner with white, angry faces. Werner was either oblivious of the sudden hostility, or chose to ignore it. He fumbled for a cigarette and lit it with a flick of a match.

Jean said stiffly, "You comprehend nothing, Mr. Werner. Nothing at all."

Werner just shrugged. "Maybe not. Who knows?"

5

The last thing that Bill Markham packed was a box of fireworks. He wrapped them carefully in waterproof cloth, then tucked them into one of the small bags labeled "Indians." He would carry thirteen such bags in the large rucksack and, looking at them, spread out round his M16 rifle and sheathed machete, he wondered how he would ever cram them all into the backpack.

The most important bag was the one with the cross: his medical supplies. He double-checked the contents. There were plenty of plasters and bandages, Paracetamol tablets and malaria pills, and of course "stop and go" pills. In the same bag were nuts, raisins, garlic and sugar: the so-called "comforts" box.

He was taking a single change of light clothing. He had a hammock, a sleeping-bag and an insect net. He double-checked the cans of insect repellent and fungal powder. As a final thought he added a second fifty-meter length of nylon cord—for crossing rivers—to the pack.

"Leave it now," Jean said. Heather had gone to bed, and Uwe

Werner was sleeping on the couch, his breathing ragged, his body restless.

"I hate leaving anything behind. I forgot my toothpaste last year . . ."

"I know. You told me."

"It's amazing how jealous someone can get about mint paste. He allowed me one squeeze every two days."

Jean smiled and surveyed the crammed bags, all of them ready to be pressed into the backpack.

"Have you got a good selection of gifts?"

Bill nodded. "Mirrors, scissors, knives, six enamel bowls . . ."

"No beads?"

"A few beads. You never know."

"Where are your spare clips?"

"For the M16? Already in. I'm taking six."

"Let's hope you bring six back."

Werner stirred in his sleep and spoke incoherently. They turned to look at him and Jean said, "Maybe I should have punched him in the mouth, for what he said about Tommy."

"Do it now."

"He probably wouldn't wake up. Maybe I should just strangle him."

"Don't do that," Bill said with a smile. "He might be having one of his lucky dreams."

As if he had heard them, and was responding to their thoughts, Werner suddenly cried out in his sleep and twisted violently on the couch. He had slapped a hand to his throat. The bushy ridge of his eyebrows twitched above his closed eyes.

Jean giggled and Bill put his arm round her shoulders. They went out on to the balcony. It was after midnight and departure time was at dawn, in order to get the *Vulcao*, a small packet ship sailing up-river to Grey's Landing. But Bill didn't feel in the least tired. He wouldn't see Jean for six weeks, and these moments together were to be savored. At the back of both their minds was the thought of the danger, and the possibility that Bill would not come home at all.

The city was alive with light. Bright moonlight made the river gleam. There was no mist this evening. A dredger was chugging its way slowly down-river, a search beam on its bridge-housing casting a yellow streak across the dark shanty town at the river's edge.

Bill had spent many hours on this balcony, when Jean had been sleeping. He had never told her of Tommy's silent cry to the Indians, his mind-call learned from a TV science-fiction show. He had never told her because, of course, it had simply been a childish game. And yet he was unable to forget the tragic irony of what Tommy had been pretending to do, and he had found himself trapped in a short, superstitious ritual of his own.

On each of the evenings before he had departed for the forest search he had stood on this balcony, closed his eyes, and called for Tommy. He did it now, without Jean being aware of it. He called for his son, imagining his voice echoing through the dark silence of the jungle, and waking the boy where he slept, bright blue eyes watching him across the vast distance . . .

I'm coming home . . .

"Let's go to bed," Jean said, breaking into her husband's thoughts.

At the very first break of dawn, Bill stepped into Heather's room and gently shook the girl awake. Heather hugged him, groggy and sad that her father was going. "Good luck, Dad."

"Keep this place in good order, now. And keep off the phone so I can get through to you when I can."

"Don't *worry*."

"Bye then, sweetheart."

"Bye . . ."

6

It was a five-mile drive to the landing stage where the *Vulcao* was moored. The packet was a tiny ship, far smaller than Werner had been expecting. Most of its above-deck housing seemed to have been built in stages, over many years, and was clumsily patched and very ragged. The grey paint was peeling from its hull, and the air in its vicinity was thick with diesel fumes as someone—below—gave the sluggish engines a pre-sailing service.

Markham led the way aboard, helped by the first mate—a solemn-faced mestizo of middle age, far more Indian than European—who waved a hand to the fore and grunted something that Markham intuited rather than understood.

"I think this is our berth," he said as Werner followed him round the deck.

"It'll do," the German said.

Their travel space, then, was the cramped area forward of the high wheel-housing. They attached their mosquito nets to the low deck rail and the housing itself. Werner pushed his pack into a comfortable position for sleeping, lay down, and pulled his wide-brimmed jungle hat over his face. "Wake me up when we leave," he said.

Markham went aft and leaned on the rail there, staring at the quayside activity, at the rows of tin and wood huts, built on stilts nearly fifty yards out into the river, and at the distant gleam of the city proper. This early, the air was still quite heavy with dawn mist, and the AmazCo building was just a dark grey finger beyond the shanty town, a red light winking on and off at its top. Intermingled with the choking fumes of burnt diesel was the smell of burnt chili. Markham didn't feel in the least hungry. Not yet. He watched the first river activity of the new day, a series of low, crude canoes pushed out into mid-stream to fish. They bobbed on the water as a log raft was tugged down-stream, then vanished into the rippling gleam of sun on the river.

He should have known that the *Vulcao* would not leave on time. Three hours after they had sleepily come aboard the craft was still moored, and some animated conversation was occurring on the landing stage. Voices were raised, hands were slapped to sides, exasperation expressed. The diesel fumes had diminished and now the air was sweet with the smell of smoked fish, and Markham's stomach began to rumble hollowly. He went forward and searched in his pack for some biscuits.

"We should have got the river plane this evening," Werner said from below his hat. "Gone up to Koume Point and taken a launch."

"I thought this would be quicker," Markham muttered.

"We can still change our minds . . ."

Before Markham could reply, however, the quayside confrontation ended. The *Vulcao*'s captain turned and leapt aboard the ship, shouted at his crew, and came forward to cast off the tethering line.

"There's some problem?" Markham asked. The Brazilian didn't

look at him, just scowled and shouted, "No whisky. No whisky for the Kanata. For the village!"

Markham pressed no further. He could grasp what had happened. There were villages all along these first miles of river, and every river captain got his supplies of coca from one or other of them, usually in exchange for a crate of cheap, probably watered, spirit. Someone had forgotten the booze. No drugs this trip.

The *Vulcao* moved out into mid-stream and picked up speed. After half an hour it had rounded the first curve of the wide river and the city was lost from view. Most of the right bank was still land that had been cleared, with the sprawling shapes of factories and industry built high upon the barren ground. For mile upon mile there was nothing on the right except smoke and dust, and the sounds of machinery eating into the earth. On the left, patches of forest mingled with the smaller buildings of villages and settlements, and the wired-off compounds of light industry, logging camps and the supporting trades . . . in particular the bars.

By mid-afternoon, however, all of this was behind them. The river narrowed and became quieter. The forest grew closer to the water's edge, and leaned more towards the channel. The trees seemed higher. Where the jungle was broken the settlements seemed less destructive, less intrusive. The river snaked more, and the noise of the packet's engines drummed back at the vessel from the confining undergrowth.

They stopped at Koume Point three hours before the river plane would have splashed down, thus vindicating Markham's decision to journey on the *Vulcao*. Koume Point was a trading-post, with a small medical facility and a large radio center. In a way it was the last stop between civilization and the brooding silence of the great Amazon Basin itself. From Koume Point onwards the river was a different world, and the forest seemed to know it and was a more vigorous and riotous growth, more enclosing, more restless.

Markham and Werner took advantage of the stop to eat, an abandoned and glorious meal of fish and fresh vegetables, followed by two or three glasses of a spirit drink distilled from manioc roots. They were relaxed and contented by dusk, and asleep soon after.

In the morning they were woken after dawn by the sound of excited voices. Markham immediately grabbed for his M16, but as he sat up below the draped insect net he realized that it was something in the water which was causing the excitement.

It was an anaconda, gliding through the river in parallel with the *Vulcao*, seemingly undisturbed by the vibration of the boat's engine. The snake must have been thirty feet long, a sinuous grey-green shape that abruptly twisted about and swam towards the shore. Markham and Werner watched it as the boat passed on. It slithered out of the water and began to wind its way into the overhanging forest. Above it, monkeys chattered hysterically and the dark shapes of four birds wheeled into the bright sky.

Uwe Werner was now in his element. All tiredness gone, his excitement grew with every mile that the packet slid deeper into the rainforest. He took two or three deep breaths, smiling and slapping his chest. Markham splashed his face with cold water from the wash-bucket. Water and air both had the same scent: decay, vegetable decay. It was not unpleasant.

"Can you smell the oxygen, Bill?" the German said, still standing by the rail and greeting the new morning.

Markham laughed. "Come on, Uwe! You know oxygen doesn't smell. That's the rot. The smell of the forest. The smell of decay."

It was Werner's turn to contradict. He wagged a finger at the American and shook his head. "Don't confuse a bad smell with a bad process. It's the scent of the forest, yes. But not just the scent of decay. It's the smell of creation also . . . look around you, Bill. Growth! Blind growth! Look at it. *Feel* it!"

Markham was amused by the anthropologist. "I had no idea you were such a romantic, Uwe. No idea at all."

Two hours later the river seemed to fork, the wide flow curving away to the north, and a narrower stretch of water joining from the west. This was the tributary known as Grey Water, and the small boat shuddered and turned, its engines working overtime against the dual flow of river, and was soon nosing into the narrow channel.

Grey Water wound its way sinuously through the rainforest. Markham sat at the prow and watched those sheer, brilliant walls of vegetation, and sensed the immensity of the world beyond vision, and the stillness of it, and the majesty. Perhaps he had caught some of Werner's romance. But mostly, as each curve in the river brought yet another green, yellow and red wall of plant life into view, mostly he thought of Tommy.

He thought of how the Smiling People must have been standing within arm's reach of him as he had prowled the edge of the forest, ten years ago. In a strip no wider than someone's back garden he had been unable to see the people who had stolen his son. How would he ever find the boy in so vast a realm—mile after mile after endless mile of tangled, luxurious, crowded growth. Blind growth, Uwe was right. Riotous creation.

The task seemed hopeless, and his stomach churned. His heart raced, and he willed it to slow. There were ways and means, he knew. He could follow hunt-trails, follow smoke signs, go to the places where he was *told* there were Indians, and he could listen to talk . . .

But for nine long years that talk, and that effort, had always led him back to a packet boat like the *Vulcao*, returning down-stream to Belore, exhausted and heavy-headed; dark of spirit.

I won't rest until we've found him. Tommy is not dead. He's just lost to us. We WILL *find him. And only then . . . an end to it . . .*

There had been a storm farther on. That much was clear from the number of branches that were floating down-stream. The journey along Grey Water was made hazardous by them, and Markham and Uwe Werner gave a hand, using long poles to push at the dangerous vegetation as it drifted by. The sound of the engine echoed dully from the forest wall and the boat was enclosed in a sound capsule that seemed to isolate it. Markham felt very cold, and very far from home. By midafternoon he was in a black mood, crouched at the front of the *Vulcao* and in no frame of mind for Werner's tactless conversation.

This was the way it always happened, however, and the German had been up-river with Markham enough times to know it. For the anthropologist the journey was an adventure—a chance to make contact with an unknown tribe and thus achieve scientific note-worthiness. For Markham it was a journey into a darker place, in search of something that was now a part of the primality of the forest. Where Werner needed to keep all his civilized faculties intact, Markham needed a time to shed layers, to remove the masks that marked him out as from the twentieth century.

"Have you ever seen a snake shedding skin?" he had said to Werner last year. "Well, that's like me. Only I don't shed skin, I shed sounds. The sound of the TV. The sound of voices. The sound of machines. The sound of the dam. Have you ever noticed how there are never any *voices* in the forest? Just a *voice*. A single voice. I go up the river and I strip away the sounds in my head until I can hear that voice."

"And what does it say?"

"It's not what it says. It's the fact of being able to hear it."

"Sounds a little mystical to me," Werner had sneered. "I thought you were the pragmatic engineer."

Markham had watched his traveling companion and felt a great deal of contempt. Looking back at the river, at the silent forest as it slipped slowly past, he had said, "You miss the point. As a romantic I thought you would have understood."

"But I do. I do understand," Werner said with a smile. "It's a psychological ritual. It keeps you sane. You 'tune in' to the forest and you begin to feel more optimistic. Closer to the earth, closer to the primitive. And your son's voice is part of the voice of the forest, and maybe you'll hear him, maybe you'll be drawn to him. Yes, I can understand why you do it. You throw off one set of masks and adopt another. But the real game is the game of 'hope.' "

Markham had twisted up with irritation at the time, but in a way Werner had been right, and so he had kept silent. Keeping his feelings to himself was very much a part of Markham's nature and it had taken some effort to talk to Werner so frankly. Werner's blunt and sardonic response had confirmed Markham's dislike of the anthropologist—but what other response than bluntness should he have expected? That, in its turn, was a part of Werner's nature.

The distance between the two men would certainly grow as Markham came "closer to the earth, closer to the primitive." But by that time the routine of the journey, and of the search, would be well established.

7

An hour before dusk, on their second day on the river, the smell of cooking made Markham straighten up from where he was sprawled on his sleeping-bag, reading. He shook Werner awake.

"We're approaching Grey's Landing."

"At last."

They packed up their kit, then stood on the prow, watching as the *Vulcao* wound its way round the last curve in the river before the trading-post. As the wall of forest edged away, so the cleared ground and small thatched buildings began to appear. By the landing jetty a crowd of children had already gathered, and they waved as the small boat chugged towards them.

The *Vulcao* had made two stops on its way to Grey's Landing for the English had founded both at small settlements of so-called "shirt" Indians, Indians who had put on the shirts of the white man. Markham had shown the arrow with its black and white feathers but at neither outpost did the Indians recognize it.

Grey's Landing, however, was a bigger settlement by far. It was both Mission and trading-post, and as such was a focus of activity for tens of miles around. It had had a long-range radio installed three years ago, and Markham had been able to contact the French priest who ran the mission and advise him of their arrival. In fact, Markham spoke to Padre Leduc about twice a year. Always the same questions: "Any new or strange arrivals? Anyone know of the Smiling People?"

The Indians who lived in the low thatched buildings around the Mission building itself changed almost as often as the wind that blew along the river. Grey's Landing was always crowded. Each hut supported a community of men, women and children, and some of those communities were regular visitors, some just passing through, shirt Indians seeking something called "prosperity," something called "civilization"; they ended up collecting latex and trading weeks of hard, wild labor for a few nights of food and shelter at a place like Grey's Landing.

But then at Grey's Landing they also got the Ten Commandments.

The Mission building was a circular hut, thatched with palm, with a smoke hole in its center, just behind the large wooden cross that reached fifteen feet to the heavens. In front of it was a wide canopy and beneath the canopy ten or fifteen Indians sat and smoked. They talked about the old ways, and the new ways, and chewed manioc roots to make into liquor, and passed time. From among them, as the *Vulcao* tethered up to the jetty, rose a tall, thin young man, dressed in white shirt and baggy grey flannels. He had a straw hat on his head, and a brilliantly polished gold crucifix round his neck. His beard was wispy and blond, but the face it half concealed was ruddy and swollen; his eyes were bloodshot, dull to look at, watery.

Padre Leduc's body was rife with entamoeba, his liver swollen and dying with malaria.

And yet the man himself was still full of vigor—youthful vigor, since the Frenchman was only thirty or so years old. He helped Markham to the rickety wooden landing stage, then tugged at Werner's proffered hand. "Welcome to Grey's Landing."

Markham looked around him. The approach to the jetty was piled with thick bundles of rubber, ready for trading. Shirt Indians wandered about, or stood watching the new arrivals, and the sharp smell of latex filled the air from the covered workshops where the raw liquid was melted into the rubber cakes, ready for transport.

"Glad to be here," Markham said. "This is Uwe Werner."

Leduc nodded at the somber-faced German. Werner shrugged and said, "I'm a confirmed atheist, I'm afraid."

Leduc thought that was very funny. He slapped Werner on the arm, winked at Markham and said, "They're confirming atheists now? I've been out of touch too long."

Markham shared the humor. Padre Leduc led the way off the jetty, then along the river shore to where several aluminium canoes were tied to a single concrete post, fifteen feet from the water. "I got your message, Mr. Markham. And this is the best I can do."

He was kicking at one of the canoes, this one with a small outboard motor and a general look of river-worthiness about it. Markham had radioed ahead to request transport for two, with packs, to go fifty or a hundred miles further up-stream. Padre Leduc had come up trumps. The small boat was ideal.

"Excellent. Just the ticket. Who do I pay?"

"You pay me."

"We'll stay overnight and leave at daybreak. If that's all right with you . . ."

The priest seemed pleased. "I'd hoped you would stay longer, but I'm glad of any company at all. You can sleep inside the Mission."

With twilight the air around the Mission became very still, but the jungle erupted into a riot of sound, mostly bird song. The sky to the west was a threatening and exquisite swirl of red and black, where storm clouds gathered over the heart of the forest. Fires burned loudly along the river's edge, and close to the trees, where groups of Indians squatted. The sparks, like streams of incandescent insects, rose straight up in the stillness. Indian voices murmured; there was laughter. Somewhere an old man sang, a deep crooning voice, accompanied by the uncomfortable rhythm of a wood drum.

Markham walked through the fading light, stopping at each group in turn. Most of them were jealously guarding their bulky blocks of rubber, but Markham put them at their ease. He showed the arrow with its distinctive flights and watched the faces that scrutinized this example of the way of life they were—theoretically—abandoning.

Group after group failed to recognize the style. They accepted cigarettes from him as they toyed with the broken-shafted weapon, sighting along it, discussing it, pointing to the pattern of rings shallowly inscribed towards the flight end. Their voices were earnest, their language sing-song, almost fluting at times. But they always passed the arrow back to the stranger, with a thin smile and a noncommittal shrug. The groups had come from all over this part of the forest. Two old men in particular seemed to hesitate as they examined the Smiling People's arrow. When they shook their heads and grinned Markham had the distinct feeling that they were keeping something back, but persistence had no effect whatsoever. They watched him, lips slightly parted to expose yellow, filed teeth, until at last he rose from his haunches and walked to the next fire.

Disheartened, depressed, Markham made his way back to the Mission hut. Inside, Werner was sitting cross-legged next to the small fire, watching the smoke rise. There were three skewers of meat roasting over the burning wood and Padre Leduc was keeping an eye on them.

Markham sat down next to the priest. He stared at the black and white feathers of the arrow as Leduc turned the skewers over the crackling flames. "No luck, I take it."

"None of them recognized the style. Or none of them were letting on."

"That wouldn't surprise me," Leduc said. He lifted one of the skewers and inspected the meat, then placed it back on the simple spit-rack. Markham noticed that his skin was wet and that he was shaking slightly. "You show an unfamiliar arrow to a shirt Indian and it can come to represent one of two things. It can be *good* luck, because it means the spirit of the people is still alive in the forest. Oh sure, they will get depressed by seeing the unfamiliar feathers. But they won't tell you, because they don't know the name of the spirit, and it would be wrong to invent it. Nevertheless, they *will* invent it: and in three months' time that group will have created yet another uncontacted, lost tribe of their own kind. The Feather People, or the People of the Broken Arrow." Leduc sighed. "Anthropologists like you, Mr. Werner, get to hear about them and suddenly we have headlines: stone-age tribes still living in Amazon Jungle. Never seen by white man. Eaters of the flesh of innocent missionaries . . ." He laughed, glancing at Markham. "This place is all about 'creation.' Mr. Werner and I have been talking about it. But it's a place of mythological genesis too. When these people leave their forest homes they begin to romance about the life they left behind. They begin to create a life that never existed, a time that was *larger* than life."

He turned the meat, which sizzled as droplets of fat burned on its browning sides.

Leduc went on, "It can also mean *bad* luck. Bad Luck Indians. Equally imaginary, equally fictitious. They are Bad Luck Indians because they have sent—through you—a sign of what the shirt Indians have abandoned. A broken arrow would be especially potent. I would imagine that that is the reason for your feeling of them 'holding back.' If they acknowledge the arrow, they acknowledge their forgotten spirits, their shadows."

Werner was watching the priest with rapt interest. Markham had heard this before. He knew very well what he was up against. The German said, "So most uncontacted tribes are simply imaginary? But that doesn't mean that a *real* unknown people doesn't exist."

"Indeed not," Leduc said. "Sometimes—in fact, *usually*—a hidden tribe is well known about, by the signs of its hunt, or its fires. That's hard evidence that can't be disputed."

"Is there any such evidence in the *makira aku*?" Markham asked.

"In the what?"

"The area to the west and south of here. The *makira aku*."

"So that's what they call it. I didn't know." He prodded the fire as he nodded thoughtfully. "That's a vast stretch of forest, and it's quite hilly. And yes, there is talk of an Indian tribe who live and hunt there. Some refer to them as the Monkey Skull people. That's their sign, and they mark their spirit trails with a monkey's head on a spear." Leduc rubbed his eyes, and wiped a hand across his face. He neither looked nor sounded well. "We're talking about three years ago, though. Nothing since."

Since Jean had thought there was evidence for *three* tribes living in the *makira aku*, Markham was surprised. But Leduc just shrugged. "I wonder what the evidence *was*? Which shirt Indian earned his keep talking about the old days of his tribe and teasing the imaginations of his listeners? One can never be sure."

It was not what Bill Markham had wanted to hear. But before he could respond to Leduc's gentle cynicism, before he could begin to search for the way in which Leduc was wrong, there came a hesitant call from outside, and the three men round the fire looked towards the open door of the hut.

The young Indian who stepped nervously inside was from one of the groups which Markham had felt were not revealing all they knew. He wore a T-shirt—printed with a picture of Bob Dylan—and what looked like a pair of swimming trunks. He had finger paint on his face and arms, and his hair was cropped short.

Leduc beckoned the youth over to the fire. The Indian approached hesitantly, dark eyes gleaming in the light. He seemed as nervous of this sanctuary as of the three white men. Perhaps, outside round the fires, the God who inhabited this place was talked of in nervous terms.

Dropping to a crouch by Markham, the youth picked up the arrow and turned it over in his fingers.

"What's your name?" Leduc asked in a dialect of Huizinga.

"Ujari," the Indian replied. He shook the arrow, looking intently at the priest, and said something so fast that Markham failed to understand the words. Ujari turned to Markham. Again he held the arrow up, shaking it, then pointing to the feathers.

This time, as he spoke, Markham grasped the sense. Or thought he did. Ujari was saying, "Being-no-seen."

"Being no seen? What does that mean?"

Leduc said, "He's saying that this arrow belongs to the Invisible People."

Ujari talked on, his confidence growing. He beckoned with his right arm, and became quite agitated at one point. His expressed agitation was as nothing, however, when compared to the excitement that Markham was trying hard not to show. But his heart was racing, and the light of the flames seemed dazzling. Ujari's voice was a symphony of sweet sound.

Leduc translated: "He says the Invisible People go for months on the hunt-trail, but he thinks they are back at their spirit grounds. He says no one ever sees them. They take the shape of macaws and monkeys, so their talk can often be heard. The arrow isn't a war arrow, it's a warning arrow. Stay away. That's how they know of the Invisible People. They are like shadows in the forest, he says. Ghosts. They have never been seen."

"Then how do they know of them?" Markham asked.

Ujari said, "The old men heard their sounds. Their guardian spirit is the spirit of an eagle and the old men saw the eagle, flying as if in a dream."

"And could these be the same as the Monkey Skull people?"

When Leduc asked the question, Ujari frowned, stared hard at the fire, and then shook his head. He spoke so slowly that Markham could understand. "The Monkey Skulls are the Fierce People. They eat the flesh and the souls of others."

The expression "Fierce People" was not a specific one. Most tribes which practiced the tradition of the eating of captives were referred to in this way. And if there were no dangerous tribes in the vicinity, then the local Indians would invent one. It was disappointing to hear that the Monkey Skull tribe were of such a nature; it cast doubt upon their real existence.

Markham asked, "Is there any knowledge of a yellow-haired boy among the Invisible People?"

Ujari shook his head.

"How do I find them?"

The Indian laughed. "Perhaps if you could fly like an eagle . . ." He shrugged. When Markham persisted, all he could say was that their hunt-trail led to the west, and that they lived on the other side of Grey Water.

Ujari left the Mission hut and walked down to the water's edge, dropping to a crouch again and watching the purple colors of dusk that were reflected in the river. Markham followed him out, but stood in the doorway, staring to the west, to the last light of the long, equatorial day. He suddenly felt very calm, as if a great crisis had passed. And yet . . . and yet it was only now beginning.

Padre Leduc stepped out of the hut and rested a hand gently on Markham's arm. "It took great courage for Ujari to come and speak with us."

"I'm sure it did," Markham said. "I'm grateful to him."

"You've waited a long time for this moment . . ."

"Yes," Markham agreed. "I'm closer to Tommy, now, than I've ever been. And yet . . . what does distance mean in forest like this?"

Leduc knew exactly what Bill Markham meant. He smiled, then shrugged slightly. "What it means is a change of tactics. A new approach to the searching." He glanced at the American. "You seem a little upset."

"Not upset," Markham said. "Stunned. And apprehensive. To be this close . . . it's going to make it very difficult in five weeks' time if we've not made contact. Very difficult."

8

They went on up the river, taking turns at the outboard motor, guiding the fragile craft between the forest debris that cluttered the water, always fighting against the powerful down-stream flow.

The jungle overhung the river bank, crowding the water, its colors exquisite, its perfume breathtaking. Full-bloomed mimosa scattered rich shades of pink among the glistening greens and yellows of the broad-leaved forest. Other blossom, blues, reds and whites, turned the vegetation into a tapestry that was sometimes almost hypnotizing in its confusion of hues and shadows.

Whenever the forest retreated from the winding river's edge to form a shallow, sandy beach, Markham led the way to shore and examined the ground for the signs of humankind. They discovered many animal spoor, but nothing that would have encouraged them to stop and make camp, calling the hidden people to them.

Nothing, that is, until the late afternoon of the second day.

The first indication of the rapids was an increase in the number of fronds of the reddish water-weed which Uwe Werner called paku-weed. It grew in profusion in the rocky shallows of the tumbling watercourses that plagued the tributaries of the Amazon. A few miles further and the water itself changed; it seemed translucent; at the shore or forest line there were thin bands of pink and white foam.

Soon the roar of the rapids could be distinctly heard above the drone of the outboard motor. Werner, who was at the tiller, swung the canoe close to the forest line. When they came round the last bend in the river he had to fight to keep the boat heading straight as they came into the deep pool, with its swirling, broken currents.

"We'll never make it up that lot!" he shouted, quite unnecessarily. Markham glanced at him coolly, as if to say, "You don't say . . ."

He pointed across the deep water. On the far side of the pool, just visible through the haze of spray and steam, the bank of the river was more accessible. The water cascaded across at least three lines of gleaming black rocks, and in the center of the deep water there was a standing wave that would be impossible to negotiate. Werner let the canoe drift two hundred yards back down-stream, then crossed the flow, and fought his way carefully to the wet sand of the shore.

Markham jumped out into shallow water and hauled the craft to safety. Both men were saturated, now, and deafened by the thundering movement of the water. The rocks over which they dragged the canoe were slick with moss and weed but they managed to get themselves, and their craft, to a place which was sheltered and still—and dry.

For the better part of an hour they hauled the boat along the length of the cascade of water, sometimes having to cut their way through the undergrowth, at other times pushing and heaving the light vessel over the dangerous rocks. In this way they traversed the full half-mile of the rapids, and sat down, exhausted but triumphant, on the narrow stretch of sand that ended the quiet stretch of river ahead of them.

A single line of footprints—bare-toed and small—traversed this bank of sand, entering the water. A deep depression in the shallows showed where the person had stood for a long time, spearing the fish that lived among the green and red weed.

Uwe Werner grinned broadly as Markham, as calmly as possible, drew attention to the markings. "I was beginning to lose faith in you," he said.

"Male or female?" Markham asked, more practically.

"Young male, I would guess." Werner watched as the depression in the sand below the shallow water was rapidly filling in. "He was here just now. We scared him off."

"If he was here just now, then he's still here," Markham said, and the two men glanced quickly at the forest behind them.

"Indeed," Werner agreed.

"We camp here. I'll construct a gift rack."

"I'll go fishing," Werner said with a smile. "Paku is delicious and this water is full of them."

By the time Markham had finished the gift rack, Werner had returned with two small fish and built a fire. The rack was a simple affair of bamboo and thin creeper. Markham selected a pair of scissors, a mirror, a pot and a necklace and tied them to the horizontal bar. They spun slowly in the dusk light, shining.

The paku fish sizzled and gave off a delicious aroma. Uwe Werner slapped his face and cursed as insects bit—more aggressive, now, as the night fell. He slung hammocks between trees and tried to drape insect netting over them to make an effective screen, but the two men were resigned to another uncomfortable night at nature's mercy.

After they had eaten—and Werner was not wrong, the weed-feeding fish were excellent—they hauled themselves into their hammocks and pulled the netting tight. The forest shrieked and whistled, apparently closing in around them, rustling and whispering as it did so. For a while every furtive movement made Werner start, peering into the darkness through his shroud. But if it were Indians approaching there would be no sound at all, and he soon relaxed.

The mosquitoes continued to bother him. "How do they get under the net? How do they *do* it?" He slapped his neck vigorously as he spoke. His reading light flashed and flickered, and Markham watched him, half amused.

"After a few years they seem to get tired of you. Or you get tired of swatting them."

"I hate them," Werner complained. He was edgy, now, anxious for something to happen. "All this waiting. Is this what you have done for ten years? Just waiting in the jungle, watching the moonlight?"

"You're not losing your sense of humor are you, Uwe?" Markham asked drily.

One of the pots rattled on the gift rack. Markham sat up as best he could, and Werner switched off his small torch. The gifts were all spinning, reflecting silver. A small dark shape passed in front of the gleaming objects and reached out to tap the mirror.

"It's just a monkey," Markham said.

"It'll take the gifts."

"I know . . ." He swung his legs out of the hammock and threw a shoe at the small creature, which scampered into the night's oblivion. Walking back to the gifts, Markham stopped them spinning, then rescued his boot. He crouched close to the water, staring back into the forest, listening hard. Then, on impulse, he went to his pack and drew out one of the sky-rocket fireworks. "It's worth a try," he said to Werner. "Maybe our fishing friend hadn't noticed us after all."

The rocket flared in the night, shot skywards on a tail of yellow sparks and exploded majestically, a spreading flower of red and blue. The gunshot sound of its destruction made Werner jump.

"That should bring them out from miles around," he said. The dead rocket splashed gently into the water a few yards away.

Markham turned back towards the small camp but hesitated, looking beyond the German. Softly he said, "Maybe they won't have to come as far as you think. Maybe they're close by already."

Werner shook his head. "You can't see Indians, but you always know they're there. Mark my words, Bill. We'll know when they've come."

"Take a look behind you, Uwe," Markham murmured. Werner glanced at him, then slowly turned. The darkness was absolute, and yet within that blackness . . . movement. The movement resolved slightly. Werner flashed his torch into the jungle, and gasped.

First one face, then two, then many resolved in the gloom. The Indians watched from the edge of the small clearing, but didn't move away from the light, nor forward into better view. Markham quickly counted the faces he could see. At least fifteen, he thought. And they were painted, and the white that decorated their faces made them look spectral and sinister.

"We'll know when they've come, eh?" Markham said, but Uwe Werner didn't rise to the bait.

He just said, "Bill, I think we're in trouble."

9

It was one of the longest nights that Bill Markham had ever known. The group of hunters remained where they were, not threatening, not withdrawing. Werner offered them the pots and the mirror from the gift rack, but there was no response. When Markham spoke to them—using the Tupi language—they made only a fractional response.

"Do they understand us?" Werner asked.

Markham said to the hunters, "Shall we make more color in the sky?" When he spoke the words, two of the younger men glanced quickly up. "They understand us," Markham said.

Werner approached the jungle's edge, then stopped. From the leaves and undergrowth behind which they stood, several bone-bladed spears had appeared. Two of the Indians hissed violently between their teeth, then were silent. When Uwe Werner backed off, two others made a brief whooping sound that echoed in the night and caused a flutter of animal activity in the high canopy.

Markham gathered dry sticks and a firelighter and made up the fire again. They had been very slack in allowing it to burn down to a dim glow. By the brighter flames the faces of the hunters took on more character, but it was not until the first crimson light of the new day that Markham was able to see the group clearly.

He had never seen tribal decoration quite like it. Their hair, cut short around the crown, was dyed a brilliant red. The skeletal effect of their faces was achieved with white and black dyes. Their naked torsos were patterned with diamond shapes, and on their limbs and round their necks they had strings of feathers and bone fragments. All the group carried the white-bladed spears, and four had blowpipes. The leader of the group had a stone club around his neck as well, and the white paint on his face was circular so that he peered out of a round mask.

"Astonishing," Werner breathed. "Truly astonishing."

Markham was well aware that the German was frightened. Werner had been shaking for most of the night, crouched by the fire, his small automatic rifle within arm's reach. Several times he had said to the American that they were in trouble. Markham had asked why.

"Because they don't move. Because they don't talk."

"Maybe they're as scared of us as we are of them."

"No," Werner said. "They know what we are. They know where we come from. They've seen people like us before. This is a ritual of some sort."

"What sort?"

"I don't know. This is waiting-for-a-purpose. This is the ritual of the *hunt* wait. Maybe. Maybe not."

"That doesn't exactly help, Uwe . . ."

"I know. What do you expect? All I know is . . . I sense danger."

Markham sensed it too. It was an indefinable feeling, an awareness of wrongness that was more than just the clash of cultures. It was the way the hunters watched them, so fixedly, so deliberately, hunters and their game . . .

And yet, this tribe might be the tribe that had taken Tommy. It was a thought that would not go away, even though these Indians were in no way representative of the Smiling People that Tommy had talked of. But ten years was a long time in the forest, and much might have happened to change the smiles of the people who had abducted the white boy.

So Bill Markham waited out the long night, as patiently as he could, as calmly as he could, as carefully as his instincts demanded.

"This is what you came for, isn't it?" he asked Werner, as dawn began to seep through the jungle.

"A lost tribe? You think so?"

"The only people lost around here is us," Markham murmured. "But these are unknown people. They speak a dialect of Tupi, I'm sure of that. But this group hasn't been contacted before. Come on, Uwe, this is the big moment."

"Every instinct I have tells me that these men are wearing war-paint."

Markham nodded his agreement, a grim, slight gesture. "Me too."

Five times Bill Markham spoke to the Indians about the white boy, Tommy, describing him, trying to indicate the number of years since his loss. Five times he was ignored.

But with the warm, heavy mists of dawn, with the sounds of the forest coming alive for the new day, so the hunters' behavior changed. They dispersed through the undergrowth and formed a full circle round the two strangers. They began to murmur rhythmically, and in their low chanting Markham heard the repeated word "Jacareh," which he took to be a name. He also heard an expression meaning "fierce," and the hunters said this in a slight shout, seemingly an affectation of pride. With a shudder of apprehension he realized that this band of Indians was the band known as the Fierce People; and it was an attributed name which they had adopted for themselves, pleased with the appellation.

As the group closed in so Markham and Werner cautiously primed their weapons, ready for a noisy and bloody escape. But the group's leader waved to them, and called for them to follow. And although the band made gestures with their bone spears, they were more in the form of encouragement than hostility.

Markham grabbed his heavy pack, but the Indians were impatient when he tried to gather up the hammocks and insect nets. Two of them picked up the gifts. One tried to touch the M16 machine rifle, but Markham discouraged the curiosity.

Quite suddenly they were moving through the deep forest, running with the hunters of the Fierce People, imitating the natives' sinuous style. The Fierce People progressed through the forest in single file. Every twenty paces they bobbed slightly. Sometimes they jumped and hopped. They made thrusting, warlike movements with their weapons, and kept up a regular chant in rhythm with their shallow breathing. With Markham and Werner in the middle, two of the Indians flanked them, and these ran in silence, watching the white men all the time.

They moved through the jungle for most of the day, weaving and dodging their way along a hunt-trail that was recognizable as little more than the least tangled route through the riot of vegetation. Uwe Werner, far less fit than Markham, was soon exhausted and in great pain; but he was too frightened to stop, and he stumbled on, the sweat pouring from his face, his clothing drenched.

In the late afternoon they heard drums, the hollow, high-pitched sound of log drums, communicating across many miles. The hunters began to chant a different journey song now, a more aggressive one, and yet a repeated cry that was uttered with smiles and a greater acknowledgment of the strangers. All the time, Markham kept his rifle ready, the safety catch off. But he smiled back and tried to talk to the hunters. He received more response, but mostly the repeated name "Jacareh." Jacareh, Werner deduced from what Markham told him, was the tribal chief, and was both beast and god in human shape.

"What sort of beast?" Markham asked. Werner, breathless and almost dropping from the pace of the march, said, "A jaguar, I think."

"Terrific."

They were in the village of the Fierce People before they realized it. They had seen no smoke, smelled no fire or cooking. One moment the jungle had been slapping and dragging at them, the next they were in a small clearing, among bamboo and palm-thatched houses. The village was almost built *on to* the forest, with huts constructed in the wide spaces between tree roots, or propped against the thick, liana-bound trunks. Markham had been expecting the classic shabano, a ringed compound with the huts round the inner wall. This place was as chaotic as the forest that crowded in upon it.

Fires burned everywhere, and the drums clattered out their irritating and frightening rhythm. Women clustered around the two strangers, seeming particularly fascinated by the tall, saturnine figure of the German. Werner moved among the small, grinning females, half amused, half concerned by their attentions.

Markham was gently pushed deeper into the village, towards a raised mound of earth, where carved wooden figures had been placed. Sitting among these idols was a muscular, solemn-faced man, wearing the skin and skull of a jaguar. The beast's grinning mouth jutted out above the red paint that liberally covered the man's forehead and cheeks.

As Markham approached him, conscious of the spears that were being half-heartedly thrust towards him, he looked around, searching for a possible escape route. He shouted to Uwe Werner that they should run to the left if things got out of hand. Werner acknowledged him. He was still being curiously examined by the younger women.

In an open shelter, close to the brooding figure of Jacareh, meat hung in fly-infested rows. The carcasses were well butchered. Markham recognized pig and skinned monkey. Just outside the shelter was a pile of red-raw bones. When he stared hard at one of the fires he could see the grey ash of bones that had been charred to destruction.

We've walked in here like lambs to the slaughter, he thought grimly. His need to find Tommy, his urgency for contact, had made him reckless in his assessment of danger.

Jacareh spoke abruptly, telling his hunters to back away from the stranger. Markham shrugged off his heavy pack, took out the small sack in which he kept his chocolate and raisins, then dropped to a crouch before the tribal leader.

"My name is Bill Markham," he said in Jacareh's tongue. "And you are the jaguar Lord, Jacareh. I greet you."

Jacareh said, "We have met men like you before. We have watched you from the edge of the World."

"You are known in the world as the Fierce People. But no man outside the world has ever met you and talked of your hunting."

Jacareh stared hard at Markham, his eyes narrow, searching. Markham held the ferocious gaze. Jacareh smiled suddenly, then laughed. His teeth were a brilliant white and he made elaborate biting motions with them. And laughed again, while around him his painted hunters murmured an almost sensuous chant.

Without breaking the stare with the man–jaguar, Markham shouted to Werner, "If they were going to kill us, would they have done it by now?"

"That's not an area in which I've had much experience," the German replied. "But my instinct now says this hostility is show. I think they may be testing our courage in several ways."

What courage of *yours* are they testing? Markham wondered silently, thinking of the inquisitive hands that were mauling and stroking Werner's body.

Jacareh said something, his voice angry. Markham caught the expression "pig words" and guessed that he was being told not to speak in that evil language.

"I have been seeking the Fierce People for many days," Markham said. Jacareh glanced at his hunters and emitted a strange sound, a brief trill that Markham guessed was humor. Jacareh looked back at him, propping his chin on his hand in an almost insultingly indifferent way. He was inviting Markham to continue.

"I'm looking for my son. A white boy with white hair. His name is Tommy. Some years ago he was taken into the world by a tribe. I want to see him again. Was that tribe this one? Did the Fierce People take the boy Tommy?"

Jacareh grinned. "All the men of the tribe are white," he said, and Markham couldn't help glancing round at the circle of white-painted faces. The hunters laughed, shaking their spears towards the crouching stranger. "But we all have *red* hair," Jacareh said, and that too seemed to amuse the Fierce People.

"Then perhaps Jacareh knows of the people who *did* take the boy. They use this arrow . . ." He reached to his pack for the broken shaft of the Smiling People's arrow and held it towards the arrogant leader. "Can you tell us which people of the world use such feathers?" He touched the black and white flights.

Jacareh exploded with laughter. He spoke rapidly and excitedly to the hunters who surrounded Markham, and the men all stepped towards the American, then backed away, raising their spears and vocally sharing in the chieftain's sudden merriment. Markham glanced quickly at Uwe Werner. The German was standing quite still, but the women and old men who had gathered around him were all watching their leader. Slowly Werner raised his hands and Markham realized what he was saying.

I haven't got my rifle . . .

Damn you, Uwe! That was just plain careless!

Jacareh rose to his feet, staring down at Markham. He touched the belt of small bones that he wore around his waist. He said, "The arrow belongs to the Invisible People."

The name made Markham go cold with excitement.

"Do the Invisible People live near here?" he asked.

Jacareh said, "Not as many of them now as yesterday." He laughed. "The Invisible People are good meat. They are very sweet. But you look even sweeter . . ."

"Uwe! Break loose!"

As he shouted the warning so Markham sprang back from where

he had been crouching. Three spears thudded into the ground. A third sailed past him and he rolled on the dry earth, came up quickly and scattered rifle fire in a short arc. Another spear struck his leg with its shaft. The hunters around him were screeching and backing away. Two of them were writhing on the ground clutching at bloody holes in their bodies. A third lay spreadeagled at Jacareh's feet, quite dead.

The Fierce People fell suddenly and uncannily silent. They crowded round Markham, ready to kill, but he could sense their hesitance. Jacareh himself barked the order that they should not harm him. Not yet.

"What's going on?" Uwe Werner asked. "Why'd they attack?"

"Guess," Markham said.

"Man-eaters?"

"Top of the class. Are you free to move?"

"I'm a little trapped. Two spears in very dangerous positions."

Sorry, Uwe. You were a little too confident . . .

One of the men at the edge of the village began to tap his log drum, but Jacareh shouted him silent. Even the birds in the high canopy seemed to have fallen quiet, shocked by the staccato roar of the M16.

Jacareh stared down at the dead hunter. He crouched by the body and touched the blood, tasted it, licking his finger wonderingly. He then smeared the blood away from the bullet hole in the man's rib-cage and pushed his finger into the wound. He probed and pushed, reaching further into the cooling flesh. He frowned as he felt something. Was it the cracked ribs, Markham wondered? Or the bullet that was wedged there?

Jacareh drew a bone knife from his belt and opened the wound wider. He reached in with two fingers, now, and after a moment drew out the bent, rust-colored metal.

He held the round up to the sky and shook his head, murmuring words that Markham couldn't distinguish. Then he licked the blood from the metal, and finally swallowed the whole thing, touching his neck as the cold object worked its way down.

He used the knife again, probing for the second bullet, raising it like a trophy and showing it to the other hunters. Then he stepped towards Markham, jerked back as Markham raised the M16, then came forward again, grinning placatingly. He crouched by the

American. He tugged at the necklace of teeth around his neck and compared the shining bullet with the shards of ivory. He spoke to Markham.

"What's he saying?" Werner called, his voice edgy and shaky.

"He says I have many teeth and the heart of a hungry jaguar. He says that in this way I am like him, and have noble ancestors. He says my dreams are a big cat's dreams, like his."

"What about me?" Werner asked desperately. Markham slowly looked round. He realized how hopeless the German's situation was. Weaponless, exhausted, he was totally surrounded by the women of the village. They were small, far smaller than the anthropologist, but they were strong, and they held his arms and his legs, giggling as he struggled, not letting go; they were as tenacious as piranha.

"Stop struggling, Uwe. I'll talk us out of this. The jaguar man is impressed by me. Take it easy . . . if the situation gets hostile again I'll just have to shoot you free . . ."

He looked back at Jacareh, who had been listening to the "pig talk" with more tolerance this time. The Indian stepped a little closer, leaning down to touch the rifle in Markham's hands. Markham tensed but let the man enjoy the cold feel of the metal. Jacareh made a strange sound in his throat, then straightened up. He stared at his fingers, at the gun, then looked round at the still writhing bodies of his two wounded hunters.

"This jaguar kills with its roar," he said to his hunters.

"The roar is endless," Markham said. He shook the rifle. "There is much death here."

He was too confused, too highly attuned to his own survival, he realized later, to have been wholly aware of what was happening. How could he have thought to have bluffed so innocent, so alien a group as Jacareh's Fierce People? Markham's reasoning was Western reasoning. Its logical consequences appeared only in his own thinking. To Jacareh he—Markham—had earned the right of death by hunt.

Werner had not.

Jacareh spoke to Markham. Werner called, "What's he say? For God's sake, Bill, what's he saying?"

Markham had turned to ice; cold, and fear, gnawed every part of him. Aloud, to Werner, he said, "They're giving me a chance. They're giving me the hunt-death. I must run, now, and at dawn they will hunt me. My God . . ."

"What about me?" Werner shrieked. "What about me, Bill?"

Markham realized it immediately, the fate that was in store for Werner. He stood quickly, bringing up the rifle and swinging quickly round to face Werner's captors. The hunters around him stepped forward, crying out in anger, raising spears . . .

But Markham just stood, frozen again, this time with shock.

Uwe Werner stared at him blindly, mouth gaping, the bloody tip of a bone spear poking several inches from his belly.

"Bill . . ." he said. "Bill . . ."

Four women stood between Markham and the German. They watched him without smiling, closing up to form a screen between the two men. Markham squeezed the trigger on the M16. A roar of gunfire broke the silence. A stream of shots flew high into the canopy.

The clip emptied. The women remained, impassive and alive. An old man cut Werner's throat and as the German's body sank to its knees so a girl collected the spurting blood in a clay vessel.

Spears pushed hard into Markham's body, breaking the skin painfully. Jacareh pointed to the emerald forest behind him and shouted. "Go, my jaguar. The hunt will begin, *my* teeth against *yours*." He held up a spear as he spoke, and grinned.

Someone behind Markham pushed him. He ran. Blindly, frantically, stumbling over his pack, but failing to get hold of it. At the edge of the village he stopped and turned back, looking to where Uwe Werner had been standing. All he could see was a group of women on their knees. They were working vigorously on the German's corpse.

How could this have happened? How in the name of God could we have let this happen to us? How could we have been so blind, so stupid?

He weaved and ducked through the jungle. He tripped on roots, stumbled on grey, moss-covered rocks, hit his head against branches, snared himself in the twining lianas that laced the forest.

When he could move no more he sank to his knees and let tears and rage pour from him. The image of Werner's dying gaze haunted him, shouted at him.

Too much obsession! Not enough care! Too much white man's arrogance, believing that innocence and harmlessness went together. He had warned his children so many times about the way the forest could turn on the unsuspecting. He had ignored his own lessons. He had pushed too hard, too fast into the unknown.

And Uwe Werner had paid for it with his life.

He fumbled in his safari suit, found a clip of bullets and banged it into the M16. He had one clip left. The rest were in his pack, back at Jacareh's village.

He moved away from the Fierce People for as long and as fast as he could. At dusk the jungle became wild, and each movement he made seemed to disturb a hundred unseen creatures. The life in the forest warbled and trilled and cried and scattered. When he found a water-filled bromeliad he quenched his thirst gratefully. He avoided eating the tempting fruits of the forest. The last thing he needed now was an upset stomach.

After dark he realized that to run further was pointless. He was so clumsy, so unaware of the hazards that the forest contained, that he would leave too easy a trail for Jacareh's hunters to follow. He found a wide-trunked tree, felt his way carefully around its soft roots and huddled in the natural cleft between one such root and the mossy ground. If there were snakes or spiders in that same sleep-space it was just too bad. He tightened his safari jacket around his throat, buttoned the cuffs, cradled the rifle between his knees and sank into a welcome, if cold and disturbed, sleep.

Every hour he woke. He began to freeze and he huddled even deeper into his clothes and into nature's arms. He grabbed handfuls of leaves and underbrush and tried to pat them round his body. Small creatures scurried and scuttled around him. Repeatedly he felt the darting touch of spidery legs across his limbs. Once, something touched his face and his cry was the loudest noise that the restless night had heard.

Before dawn he was awake. Accustomed, now, to the tropical and forest dark, he managed to pick his way carefully through the tangled jungle. He felt refreshed and alert. He was hungry, but not to the point of distraction. The worst problem was his bowels. He finally dug as deep a hole in the ground as he could manage, functioned, then tried to cover all trace of this erstwhile camping site.

Any hunter, he knew secretly, would spot the marks of his presence without hesitation.

He had to find the river . . . any river. He would take a chance with water-snakes and piranha . . . in a river he could swim rapidly with the flow and perhaps fetch up out of range of the man-eating hunters. It was—he realized—his only real hope. But Jacareh had set him running away from the river along which he and Werner had navigated themselves into trouble. And during his frantic escape the night before he had lost his direction, and could not now easily guess which way he should turn to retrace his steps.

Sunlight, breaking through the canopy, gave him an approximate idea of where the east lay. But the high canopy played strange tricks with light. Markham's dawn world was a fetid place, a warm place, a breezy place; it was a realm of yellows and greens that shifted and glimmered and occasionally blinded him with the directness of their reflected sun.

An hour after dawn he stopped and listened hard. Ahead of him he could hear a rushing sound, like water . . . like a river.

He ran frantically towards it, but emerged into a stand of tall bamboo, which was rustling and quivering in a forest breeze, an eerie and unwelcoming oddity in this primeval landscape.

He skirted the thicket. The ground cleared slightly and he realized he was on an animal trail. The droppings were large, but he was unskilled in the recognition of such things. He followed the easier track gratefully, however, then cut off to the west, scratching himself badly on thorns, and trying to see against the flashing glare of sun for another rain-swollen bulb of bromeliad.

Again he stopped. Again he listened. Again he was puzzled by a sound he could hear, but a sound from behind him, this time. It was a hissing noise, a regular, rhythmic hissing . . .

"My God . . . so soon . . ."

He ran again, now. He ran for his life. If he was cut or bruised, as he weaved and ducked and blundered through the forest, he was unaware of the wounds. All he could hear was the sound of his breath—and from behind him the hissing chant of the hunters, the rhythm of their approach, their growing excitement as the scent of their quarry grew stronger.

Markham stumbled, but pushed himself to his feet again, spinning round to see what was behind hin. He saw white and red faces watching him from the green undergrowth. Shapes passed through his vision, weird, human forms, colored in bright, dazzling ways, but always with the core of skeletal white, the image of bones painted on their flesh.

An arrow grazed his arm. Two more clattered into the branches of a tree close by. He fired a short burst in a wide arc. Leaves fell, the air screamed. There was movement on both sides of him. He could see nothing.

He thought of Jean as he ran, now. He thought of Heather. They would wait for him and he would not return. They would hear from Padre Leduc that he had reached Grey's Landing safely. They would hear of the Fierce People. They would know what had happened . . . they would never quite believe it, and they would never stop waiting . . .

As the moment of his death padded closer, as the sound of demons grew louder in his mind, he became very sad. He was without feeling as he ran, unaware of the pain in his body. He twisted and turned through the terrible forest, firing the M16, shooting at everything that moved.

Fear of death choked him. His eyes were blurry with tears. He found himself thinking of the earliest moments of his life with Jean, and she was very close to him, now, and memory of her was a great comfort and a great strength.

Somehow he managed to place the last clip of bullets into the breech of the rifle. When he shot the gun, men screamed.

But they were always around him. They were always there. Their faces were blooms in the bushes, their eyes the bright points of sunlight that watched him in his crashing passage to his final moment.

An arrow struck his back, but didn't penetrate his heavy jacket and shirt. Another snagged on the leather strap of the M16, and he snatched it away. Around him the sound of the hunters was a heavy striking of wooden spears on wooden bows, punctuating the regular vocal chant with which they abused and taunted their prey.

A hunter appeared before him, arrow at full stretch in its short bow. As the arrow was released so Markham shot a burst of fire, and the Fierce hunter spun backwards, his white bones reddening in a line across his chest. The arrow struck Markham's arm and he yelled and winced with the pain. But the wound, if bloody, was only superficial.

A moment later his feet went out from under him. He fell through the air for a second, then bounced and slid down a steep slope. Rocks bruised him, thorns tore at him. He clutched at a root, but the fragile wood broke. He slid another few yards—towards the rushing of water.

He hung suspended for a second more, his right hand gripping the gun, his left snagged in a forked piece of root or branch. Something gave and he tumbled, striking the water feet first.

The small river flowed vigorously to his left, passing through the deep pool of a waterfall before curving out of sight. The waterfall was high, a magnificent cascade of white- and green-lit liquid, that spumed as it struck the pool and evaporated into a heavy, lingering mist.

Within that mist a human shape was crouched, but Markham didn't notice it for a moment as he stumbled on the slippery rocks and tried to work his way with the current towards the implied safety of the gushing curtain of water.

Arrows and spears struck the river around him. He glanced up just once and saw the restless dark shapes of the Fierce People. He saw Jacareh, larger, more evil than the others, grinning through a painted mask of red and white terror.

Markham shot up at him. The clip of bullets emptied. Even so, he couldn't bring himself to let go of the metal weapon.

He staggered towards the waterfall. The figure that crouched there rose to its feet and Markham saw it. It was a young Indian. He was decked in armlets and a necklet of bone and feathers. His face was painted in green spirals. His arms were striped red. He was otherwise quite naked. His hair was dyed yellow . . .

Man and youth stared at each other for a split second, and in that moment of hesitation Bill Markham had swung round his empty rifle and squeezed the trigger. That simple, violent action evoked a response from the Indian by the pool. He let loose an arrow at the stranger, and Markham flung himself to the right, and felt the wind of the wood shaft close to his ear.

When he looked back, the green-painted, yellow-haired Indian was running towards him through the water, screaming at him, frantically nocking a new arrow into the short bow he carried.

Helpless, and weakened by loss of blood, Bill Markham turned away from the moment of his death.

PART THREE

Light of the Forest

1

The eagle had returned. It circled high above the enclosure, riding the warm air that rose from such wide clearings in the dense forest. At times it flew vigorously to the south, but in just a few heartbeats it was back, its head cocked as if it watched the scurrying activity of the Invisible People, below.

The old man Wanadi watched the eagle in wonderment. This was its fifth appearance in as many days, and he had no doubt, now, that it was being called. In the ash and dust of his hearth space he drew the shape of the eagle, and within the outline of its wings he placed two feathers, one white, one black. He sprinkled the bone ashes of his ancestors in the outline of the head then bent close to the image, listening for the ghostly whispers that might identify the source of the eagle's calling.

"A child," the spirits said to him. A child! Wanadi smiled. Of course it was a child. It would be one of the young boys, those few who were already learning the ways of the dreamlight, and of the forest. In less than three hunt-times they would begin the terrible journey that would end in their deaths, consumed by the forest . . .

Wanadi put on his necklet of eagle feathers, and his earrings of snake bone, and smeared ash eyes on his chest, a simple pattern that would take the spirit sight of his ancestors with him as he walked about the village. He looked up at the eagle again. Such a strange bird, he thought. It had gold on its neck, but its head was black. Its wings, spread wide, were tipped with white. It rocked in the sky, like a canoe on fast water, but always it was overhead.

Leaving his place below the palm thatch of the circular enclosure, Wanadi walked out into the compound, among the pigs and chickens that pecked and grubbed in the soft ground. Four fires burned around the village and most of the women were gathered about them, preparing cassava bread or manioc soup. The men made arrows, bows and spears, or applied the various poisons which the tribe used to the hunting and war darts.

Wanadi's youngest wife, Caya, came in from the forest carrying an armful of fruit. The girl smiled at him. She had not yet had his child; her eyes were bright and wide, like her smile. Her hair was long and richly dark, her belly plump. The sight of her made Wanadi sigh and think about the hammock, but Caya saw the glint in his eye and walked quickly away from him, glancing back over her shoulder with that mischievous look of hers.

Anyway, he was many hunt-trails old. He was wrinkled and losing his teeth, and Caya's attentions were burning his bones to ash before their time. It was just as well.

This brief exchange was watched by Wanadi's first wife, Uluru. She was crouched with the oldest and most wise of the women, Kura, chewing manioc roots and spitting the pulp into a large clay dish. Her third child lay across her breasts, happily asleep. Kura said something and the two women laughed. Wanadi didn't hear the rude comment, but he scowled anyway, then made an improper gesture of invitation to Kura, who roared with laughter again, exposing her toothless gums, white with manioc pulp.

Outside the enclosure, in the cleared space before the tangle of forest began, other animals were rooting for food, scurrying away from the women who were piling up wood for the fires. Children played here, too, their cries and laughter bright in the hot day. Wanadi walked about the outside wall of the village until he saw the three boys he was seeking.

They were watching the eagle. Little Mapi, his hair dyed red in a childish copy of the hunter's style, was blowing his toy blowpipe at the circling bird and making cries that mimicked the success yell of a hunter. Mapi was small for his age, and innocent, and would not undertake his hunt-death for some time. His brother, Jani, was beckoning and calling to the eagle, as if the majestic bird could see his greeting and would come and perch upon his shoulder. Wanadi knew instantly that the eagle had been summoned by neither of these.

The third boy was his own son, and Wanadi felt a thrill of both joy and fear as he saw what Tomme was doing. Tomme was taller than his friends, but strangely thin. He was two or three hunt-trails away from his initiation in the forest, his first death. His bright yellow hair, chopped off around the crown of his head, was streaked with green. He stood with his arms outstretched. He moved his arms slowly, like the eagle's wings above. Wanadi realized that his son's eyes were closed. The boy swayed slightly, then turned. Wanadi looked into the sky.

The eagle was turning.

Tomme cocked his head, then mimed a swooping motion. The eagle above him veered sharply and swooped through the blistering air, rising again on the up-draught . . .

And Tomme slowly rose from a crouch, an elegant motion, his mouth open in pleasure as he imagined himself to be flying.

Wanadi watched all this and felt pride, and sadness too. His son, then, was the eagle caller. What a great man he would be when the flush of youth was burned away. What power would be Tomme's in the hunt-times to come, after his own hunt-death.

Wanadi's grandfather had been an eagle caller. Wanadi had seen the power in only one other child, but the Fierce People had taken and eaten that child before the hunt-death, and there had been a long time of bad luck for the tribe. Wanadi had led the hunters to the edge of the World afterwards, and it was there, looking out into the wilderness, that his son Tomme had been shown to him.

That had been eight hunt-trails ago, and the boy was still haunted by the ghosts from beyond the edge of the World. But his having called the eagle meant that at last the restless bone dust that was Wanadi's ancestors had accepted the boy. Tomme was so much wiser than the other children. He was strong in ways that were usually associated with the very old. His hair remained the color of sunlight on the dead ash of a burning.

"Tomme, Tomme," Wanadi breathed, watching his son mimic the eagle. "When the time comes for you to drink my ashes in your milk, my spirit-hunt will never end. Never."

2

In the evening the fires on all nine hearths burned high. Tomme sat close to his father, watching as the old man stared thoughtfully into the open compound of the village. Wanadi's wives talked quietly. Uluru was in her hammock, playing with the infant.

After a while Wanadi went to his own corner of the covered hearth space and from a rolled blanket drew out his feathered spear. Tomme watched him excitedly. He could feel that things were changing between himself and his father. Ever since the eagle had come, Wanadi had been behaving strangely, watching his son very closely. He had continually asked him about the ghosts in his head, and Tomme had become confused, trying to remember things that would no longer be remembered.

"These are my hunt-trails," Wanadi said, as he sat back down by the fire. "This was my first . . ." He touched the tiny green feather at the top of the spear.

"Why is that feather so small?" Tomme asked.

Wanadi grinned. "It was a very small hunt. I went with my father. We caught monkeys, many monkeys. That was before my hunt-death. After that, I went with the men on the long trails, and these feathers show each of those journeys. This one . . ." he touched the black feather that was eighth from the end. "This was the trail when I found you. Because of my joy at finding you I have added a white feather on the other side of the spear." He twisted the thin shaft to show the boy. Then, running his fingers down the greens and reds of the macaw feathers, he said, "These others were just good hunts. There are twenty-four of them. That makes me the oldest man I have ever known." He chuckled at his joke, then winked at Tomme. "My ancestors have given up waiting for me. They've joined me by the hearth. Do you see?"

As Tomme shuddered at the idea of the ghostly spirits huddling under the palm thatch, he saw the ash at the edge of the fire blowing in strange spiraling patterns. His eyes widened and he licked his lips apprehensively.

Wanadi just grinned at him.

"Nobody should be frightened of ghosts," he said. "Especially not a boy with so many ghosts in his head!" He ruffled Tomme's fair hair as he spoke, and Tomme grinned.

"I have a new one," he said. "I dreamed it, last night."

In her hammock, Uluru turned to watch her son. Caya and Pequi, both sucking noisily on pineapples, crowded a little closer to hear

Tomme's new tale. Tomme—while technically their son—was only a little younger than Caya, the youngest, and Wanadi tended to treat them all as equal. It irritated Pequi, who was six hunt-trails older than the boy, and she rarely talked to him; but she was as intrigued, and amused, by Tomme's strange memories as all in the village.

"I dreamed that I was in a high place, the same high place where my ghost father and mother live. The World was so far away that I could only see it as a thin green shape on the other side of the wilderness. But I found a strange pair of eyes. They were cold to touch, from some giant animal. When I put these eyes to my own I saw the World come closer. With these eyes I could travel over the fires of the wilderness people and look into their hearths."

Caya applauded loudly as Tomme grinned and settled back on his haunches. Pequi sniffed loudly and looked away. Uluru crooned as she stroked the new baby's hair.

Wanadi nodded thoughtfully, watching his son. "Pansu would have liked that story," he said. Pansu was his third son, who had been killed and eaten by the Fierce People. His other, older children—a boy and a girl, both by Uluru—were eating at their friend's hearth tonight. Pequi's first child had died, but she now nursed her second. Wanadi's hearth was not populated tonight, and Tomme wished that more of the family had been there to hear his strange dream.

Tomme loved to tell stories. Most of the boys of his own age had no idea how to tell tales and relate their dream adventures. Wanadi had already told Tomme that it was traditional for the older folk to be the storytellers, but that because of his origins, in the wilderness, he would not be bound by the traditions. Not in the respect of storytelling, at least.

In most other ways Tomme was treated the same as the other youngsters. He was punished if he infringed the tribal laws; he was shown no favoritism. For the first two hunt-trails that he had been on with the Invisible People, the other children had been frightened of him. With his blue eyes and blond hair he was like a ghost, and with his strange words, and strange memories, he was like a wilderness monster.

Mapi, who was now his best friend, had been terrified of him, and had nicknamed him White Snake Monkey, an insult that had caught on quickly and made his first years with Wanadi's people truly miserable.

Uluru had been both friend and mother to him. She had nursed hin when he had suffered from fever, she had cradled him when he had cried—and he had cried so desperately—and had been the first to understand the strange words he spoke, and to help him learn the language of the World.

Now, Tomme was a fluent speaker, and had forgotten most of the words from his wilderness days. But he remembered enough to play a teasing game with his friends. He could invoke the old words, as he said, to control things. He knew the wilderness names for fish, and trees, and animals, and even human beings.

When he and Mapi—and the other boys—would go fishing, or hunting small snakes, Mapi would always ask him to say the strange words for things. Tomme couldn't always remember, and he usually remembered by chance. Once, when they had been climbing a tree towards the canopy, there had been a sky thunder, and sound that had frightened the boys.

"An aircraft," Tomme had said, and then wondered at the strange sound of the word.

During the years, Wanadi began to place the important words into Tomme, marking them on his body in paint, as one day they would be marked into his skin.

There were the names of the animals of the hunt, and these would soon be marked upon his chest. There were the laws of marriage and producing children, and these would be marked upon his belly. There were the names of the great forest deities, and of these the Great Anaconda was the most important, although in Wanadi's tongue it was called *ana kundar*. These names would be tattooed upon his arms, each represented by its pattern.

Tomme learned the pattern-form of these things, and practiced drawing them in the dust. He stitched and painted his first penis sheath, a rather ungainly piece of clothing which caused much laughter among the women of the village.

Most recently of all he had learned the dances of the tribe: the hunt dances, the courtship dances, the dances and chants with which the life of the tribe was changed according to good and bad fortune.

Now, too, he learned the silent songs, the ancient songs—uttered under the breath—which could draw all manner of beasts and birds into view; and not just beasts, but wind and rain and even the sun, the heat of the World.

The only thing that could not be called was the green stone that Wanadi called the "Light of the Forest"—mysterious and elusive. For all of hunt-time (and even from before the dreamlight), there had been a war between humankind and the wraiths who scattered the Light of the Forest. To own the Light of the Forest was to own a fragment of the unseen world of the ancestors.

In truth, every member of the village owned one of the green stones—which Tomme, in his old tongue, called *emeralds*—but it still made a good story, and a good quest for the youngsters who had gone through their hunt-deaths.

Wanadi said, "In the days of the dreamlight, the Great Anaconda came slowly to the forest, journeying from the north. When at last she stopped she had cut a great river through the land. In time she produced young and where those young moved away into the World they too left rivers behind them, and these are the rivers along which the people travel as they hunt."

"Were there people in the World at that time?" Tomme asked, intrigued.

"Yes," Wanadi said, after a moment's thought. "But they were much smaller than us. They lived high in the canopy and moved about the World along the branches of the trees. They made houses out of the swollen flesh of the flowers which gather water. They rarely came down to the forest floor. Only when the beings from the dreamlight had found their new places in the World did the people come down from the canopy and begin to grow, to become as we are now. As the people grew, the creatures became smaller: the snakes and monkeys, the pigs, the macaws, the jaguars and the spiders. But if you search hard enough—" he leaned forward and tapped Tomme on the knee as the boy listened, rapt and excited—"if you search hard enough, you will find the first creatures. They look like hills, or great trees, or rivers. They sleep now, which is why we have the dreamlight. But one of them will be woken when it is your time to die . . ."

Tomme shivered. "Which one will it be?"

Wanadi shrugged, then grinned at Uluru. "The way he eats, maybe we should wake the pig . . ."

"No!" Tomme said.

Wanadi hushed him gently, a finger on his lips. "For you, Tomme, for you who have called the eagle, it will be a powerful beast that will be raised to take you from this life to the life of men."

3

The time came for his first hunt.

His father shook him awake before dawn. They walked through greyness and mist to the river, and the deep pool, where they bathed. They shivered as they stepped out into the growing day. Around them the forest began to come alive with bird song and animal cries. The mist began to lift.

With the first streaks of red in the sky above them, Wanadi rose to his feet from where he had been crouched on the river bank. Water still dripped from his long hair. Tomme's cropped, blond thatch was almost dry.

Wanadi raised his arms and stared up at the heavens. Tomme mimicked the gesture and spoke the words that Wanadi spoke.

"We are naked. Today we will hunt. Tomme will make his first kill in the name of the hunt. The killing will be swift and without pain. If it is not, then may the pain be taken by Wanadi, since Wanadi has trained him. We will take only what we need. It will be a little hunt to mark the beginning of the man in the boy."

They went back to the village, then, and crouched around the cold hearth. Around them, the people were stirring. Wanadi made up the fire, a few twigs; a small fire which would be kept in until the evening, when it would be made bigger.

They dressed in simple loincloths, made of oil-softened bark. Then Wanadi tied armlets of colored feathers around Tomme's thin biceps. He placed a necklet of feather and bone over the boy's head and ran his fingers, laced with green dye, through Tomme's hair, so that the blond locks stuck up, stiff and colored. For earrings they chose long loops of stiffened animal fur, which had been painted with bright dyes. These would not rattle like the loops of painted bone that the tribe more usually wore. A porcupine spine through the boy's nasal septum formed the last part of Tomme's hunting outfit.

After Wanadi had dressed himself with feathers—mainly, a brilliant pair of red tail feathers inserted into his own nose—he showed Tomme how to paint the patterns of pursuit upon his body, and the marks of appeasement for the forest. This was the same green dye finger-painted on to the body in a series of intricately interwound spirals. When Wanadi had painted Tomme, Tomme painted his father, and the old warrior criticized and shouted, and resorted finally to directing Tomme's hand himself.

But at last it was done. They painted black rings around their eyes—to hide their eyes from the animals which they would pursue—and picked up the weapons of the hunt.

As he ran from the village, a few paces behind his father, Tomme felt enormously proud. He glanced back and saw Uluru, his mother, watching him. She waved to him, but he looked quickly away. From his own hearth, Mapi emitted the sound of a jaguar, and Tomme grinned and kicked his heel, a silent, almost invisible joke message to his friend.

Mapi would have to wait a hunt-trail more for his own first hunt, and it had been a brief source of conflict between the two boys. Mapi, though, was now over his disappointment.

The group of springtail monkeys was moving west, through the middle canopy. The older and wiser males were flanking the main group, and making much noise. This would divert attention from the young, and the females, who moved silently and stealthily across the horizontal landscape of branches.

The ploy might have fooled a big snake or a small cat, but it couldn't fool the human eyes which watched from below.

Hardly moving, Wanadi and Tomme watched the group pass overhead. Hardly speaking, Wanadi asked Tomme which would be a good kill, and Tomme said—his voice a murmur of breeze in the forest—"The small male at the end of the group."

Wanadi nodded his agreement. Full-grown, the animal was not yet of full importance to the group. It was not paired, and was probably a semi-outcast.

Its meat would taste just as sweet, however.

Tomme held the small poisoned dart towards his father. The

dart's feathered flights were green and purple, and Tomme had made them himself. Wanadi shook his head, and instead passed Tomme the tall blow-pipe. The weapon was half again as high as the Indian. Tomme reached for it, inserted the dart, then carefully raised it to his lips, struggling a little with the cumbersome pipe.

He aimed at the springtail, blew a sharp breath, saw the feathered dart strike the animal on the side.

The monkey continued to move steadily through the middle layers of the forest. It stopped and peered down, but seemed otherwise unharmed.

Tomme frowned his concern, but Wanadi just grinned, then pointed a wrinkled finger upwards again.

After a few seconds the monkey stopped and began to wobble. It behaved as if it was drunk. The rest of the group scattered quickly as the victim began to thrash in the foliage, and then dangled from a branch by its prehensile tail. It hung there for twenty heartbeats, then plummeted to the earth, quite dead.

Tomme was exhilarated. He ran to the crumpled body and mocked it. But Wanadi spoke to him sharply. "You mock a dead enemy. The monkey is not our enemy."

Chastened, Tomme looked back at the animal. "I'm sorry, father. I'm sorry, *gorozu*."

Looking down at the body too, Wanadi said, "*Gorozu*, it is with great sadness that I have taken your life. But my poison was good and you did not suffer."

"*Gorozu*," Tomme said, "I too am sad. I promise to make good use of you. Your skin will be my first pouch. Your bones will be my first arrowheads." He looked up at Wanadi, uncertain as to whether he should say more.

Wanadi sighed impatiently, but smiled at his son. "The flesh, Tomme. What will we do with the flesh?"

"*Gorozu!* We will eat your flesh in a great feast!"

Now Wanadi was satisfied. Tomme reached down and picked up the monkey, slinging it over his shoulder. He began to walk confidently back towards the village, which was several hours' walk away.

But Wanadi hissed him silent and still. The old man touched his shoulder, and pressed, so that Tomme dropped to a crouch.

Wanadi's eyes were wide with alarm. Tomme listened hard, but could hear only the rustling of creatures in the undergrowth, and the babble of bird song and raucous shriekings from above.

Wanadi tugged at his son and the two men became Invisible People, melting into the background greens and purples, even though they were hardly covered at all.

And then Tomme heard the sound that had alarmed Wanadi. It was a regular, rhythmic hissing, the eerie and menacing sign of the Fierce People.

There were twelve of them, all hunters. They loped through the forest in single file, jumping fallen trees, snaking around the denser underbrush, weaving and ducking as they picked their way along the narrowest of trails.

The line of warriors passed within an arm's length of where Tomme stood. Not even the boy's eyes moved as the twelve men ran past. But he was aware of every detail about them, from the black and red paint patterns on their bodies to the bright, feathered head-dresses that they wore. They carried the weapons of war, not the hunt.

They were seeking human prey.

When they had gone from sight, but were still audible, Wanadi motioned Tomme out of hiding. The two of them began to run along a parallel course to the Fierce People.

Wanadi wished to be sure that their target was not his own village. If it was then there would be bloodshed before the day was finished, and the fires would burn the bones of too many of the people before the morning.

They ran fast through the forest. The Fierce People were traveling at a steady, unceasing pace, and Wanadi and Tomme were soon ahead of them. They watched the glades and clearings, which had been formed by a falling tree, and the hunters snaked through the brightness without losing their rhythm. They stood by the trails formed by animals and the warriors loped past them, hissing the name of the creature that had formed this track.

At last it was clear that the Fierce People were moving in the general direction of the village. They would soon reach the river, and from there it was just a short way to the enclosure.

Wanadi knew that once this hunting band was over the water

they would soon detect the signs of the village. But he was sure that the band did not *know* that the village was there. They were on a seek-hunt.

Leading the way with all the speed and agility of a man half his age, Wanadi reached the river. Tomme was quite breathless, and dropped to a crouch by the water's edge for a moment.

When he had recovered his breath he stood up and began to step into the water. Wanadi stopped him. The old man pointed across the stream, to where the water's surface seemed to shimmer silver.

Tomme frowned, not immediately understanding. Wanadi took the dead monkey from his shoulder and held it out across the water. He held it by its tail and lowered the head below the surface.

The patch of silver shifted and moved rapidly towards the opposite bank. When it reached the monkey's corpse, Wanadi was nearly toppled by the sudden ferocious tugging from below. The water bubbled and boiled, and the silver resolved into a myriad small, sleek shapes, darting and lunging at the dark furred creature.

"Piranha!" Tomme breathed, horrified at how close he had come to stepping among them without noticing.

Wanadi wrenched the monkey up. The head was just a skull, now. Two of the tiny fish were still attached to the neck, but they fell away, glistening jaws still working.

"How do we get across?" Tomme breathed. He turned and listened behind them, but there was no sound, yet, nor a sight of the Fierce People.

Wanadi swung the monkey down-stream a few yards. The water boiled around it. A thousand tiny killers tore and snapped at the cold flesh. The two Invisible People then walked safely across the river, swimming as they reached mid-water, and dragging themselves safely and gratefully out on the other side.

"Thank you, *gorozu*, for keeping the little ones busy," Tomme whispered as they concealed themselves in the jungle again.

He had said only that when the screen of vegetation across the river broke, and the twelve hunters appeared.

Their leader was a bulky and ferocious-looking man, only half Wanadi's age, by his appearance. He clutched four spears and a long bow, with a sheath of thin arrows slung over his back. His headdress contained jaguar skin. His chest and belly were marked with red paint in a way that suggested he had been cut open. It was a taunting and defiant body pattern. I am cut open and still I live!

This man saw the remains of the monkey, still immersed in the turbulent water where the piranha finished their meal, and he led his group swiftly towards it, watching carefully from the shore as he loped alongside the drifting carcass. In this way the Fierce People were taken some hundred paces or so away from Tomme and Wanadi. At last, though, the hunters seemed satisfied. With the piranhas so involved they could cross the river safely.

Wanadi sighed with irritation, then quickly nocked an arrow into his long bow. He checked the direction and strength of the wind, then leaned back and drew the bow until the gut string almost sang with tension. He released the arrow, and almost immediately nocked a second.

Tomme watched the first arrow as it vanished high into the sky, above the river. It flew far beyond the Fierce People, and then the wind took it and turned it back! It hit the river bank close to the leader of the twelve hunters, startling him. Wanadi's second arrow, fired more directly, struck the bank a man's length away from the first. The twelve hunters ululated their alarm, and scattered, half of them hiding, the other half preparing their own bows and scanning the forest for the enemy.

The leader stalked towards the two arrows, inspected each, then snatched them from the ground and arrogantly slotted them into his own quiver. But he stayed where he was, staring hard up-stream, uncannily close to where Tomme and his father were hiding.

"Why did you shoot your arrows like that?" Tomme whispered.

"The arrows say, 'We are many. Go back. We are ready to fight . . .' "

Tomme understood immediately. The two arrows had arrived from different directions, implying a wide spread of the people from across the river, a wide band of warriors waiting for the hunters.

But the leader of the Fierce People had seen through the ploy. The way he had taken the arrows for himself implied that he was not convinced, that he still did not believe that his killing party had encountered a tribe that outnumbered them.

But he was worried. He was worried because he couldn't *see* the other warriors. There were none to see, of course, but this Indian was trying to decide whether or not he was genuinely facing a small army of the Invisible People . . . or whether he was up against a small band trying to put him off the scent.

Wanadi smiled, hushing Tomme who was expressing his alarm.

"We'll try something else . . ." he said. He cupped his hands to his mouth and emitted a loud, a piercingly loud cry. It was neither a growl nor a moan. It was a sound that Tomme had heard before, but he couldn't place it.

The Fierce People reacted instantly to the cry, then turned as the cry was answered from slightly down-stream. Wanadi grinned. Again he made the call. This time the response came from several places around the forest. The jungle seemed to bristle with tension, fluttering and rustling and falling strangely quiet.

The Fierce People watched the forest across the river, then slowly backed away into concealment. Soon only the leader was left. He stood upright, facing the jungle. He raised his arms and shouted something, a taunting challenge to the unseen foe. Then he nocked one of Wanadi's arrows and shot it back. He stood and waited, tempting fate, inviting death. He called again. It was hard for Tomme to hear exactly, but the tone of the cry was obvious enough. Nevertheless, the leader did not cross the water, nor did he bring his hunters back. He followed them into the green oblivion.

Tomme was astounded. "They believed there were many of us. Father! You are skilled in the secret ways. You *must* train me too . . ."

"Maybe," Wanadi said quietly.

Tomme was still puzzled by what had happened. "That was not our battle cry. It was like the call of a female monkey . . ."

Wanadi chuckled, gathering up his weapons. "In fact, the cry of a female monkey *in heat*!"

Tomme listened to the cacophony of sound in the forest. The cries of the monkeys—that had convinced the Fierce People that each was being emitted by a warrior—continued unabated. The canopy shivered with the violence of attraction: males to the plaintive voice of a needy female.

"Time to go," Wanadi said.

"We can kill another . . ." Tomme said.

"We can hunt on the way home. If the monkeys come like this, what else will come, do you think?"

Tomme didn't grasp his father's meaning for a moment, but then realization came, and with it a terrible shiver of fear. "Jaguars, pumas, anacondas . . ."

"Exactly." Wanadi straightened up and grinned at his son, who was almost as tall as him. "Stay if you want. But me—I've got three wives . . ."

Somewhere close by a monkey screeched as it was taken by a cat. The whole forest was electric with fear.

Tomme grabbed his blow-pipe. "Lead the way, father."

4

By the time they reached the village the forest had smiled upon them. Tomme had killed two armadillos and a wild pig, and there was some excellent eating on both of those creatures. Wanadi had shot three richly colored birds, a majestic toucan among them. These would be used to make Tomme's first head-dress. Wanadi, too, had killed the puma which they had heard killing the monkey, back by the river. He had skinned it. It would make a fine present.

Three women, gathering fruit in a clearing just beyond the village, shouted their greeting to the returning hunters. Wanadi ignored them, but Tomme smiled and held up his prizes. One of the women was the daughter of Samanpo. She was older than Tomme, but was not yet married. Her copper skin was lighter in tone than the other young women of the village, and there was scurrilous talk of the two "pale-skinned ones" becoming husband and wife.

As he looked at her, Tomme felt his face grow hot. When he looked sharply away, the girl laughed.

Inside the village, the men left off arrow- and pipe-making and came over to Wanadi's hearth to congratulate Tomme formally on his first "little" hunt. Tomme felt proud. He was a tall boy, taller than several of the adults, and today he had taken the first confident step towards full maturity of spirit.

The greetings lasted only a few minutes. There would be greater celebrations after his hunt-death. As Wanadi sat down in his hammock, with his brother and another of the elders crouched before him, Tomme looked for his friends.

Mapi ran over to him and prodded the wild pig. He was smiling broadly, but looking a little anxious. All the children were allowed to kill pigs if they saw them. *And* armadillos. It was the bigger creatures, and the monkeys which were forbidden to them.

"I killed a monkey, though," Tomme said. "It was a great monkey. One of the old males of the group. You should have seen it. Nearly as big as you, Mapi . . ."

Mapi looked at his friend quizzically. "Then where is it? Where is it? Nobody would leave a monkey in the forest . . ."

"I sacrificed it to the river. The piranhas got it. And my father and myself were able to cross the river . . ."

"You mean you *dropped* it in the river!" Mapi said, his voice gently taunting.

Tomme grabbed his friend by the shoulders and hissed at him angrily. "We were fighting the Fierce People! There were twelve of them. They were seek-hunting. We shot arrows to warn them off, and the monkey was given to the piranhas as an offering, to keep the Fierce Ones on the other side."

Mapi was impressed. "You saw the Fierce People . . . ? and you're still alive . . . ?"

Tomme nodded grimly. "We fought very hard. We convinced them that we were many. They won't come across the river, now."

Wanadi said sharply, "Enough talk of the Fierce People, Tomme. Later we shall chew tobacco and discuss the situation. Don't you have a present for someone . . . ?"

Tomme had almost forgotten. He reached to his waist where the sticky pouch made of leaves was slung. Lifting the package from its binding he walked quickly over to his hearth, where Uluru was watching him, her face brightening as she realized the gift was for her.

"We found this not far from here," Tomme said, offering her the leaf bag.

"Honey!" Uluru said delightedly. She licked her sticky fingers, then sucked at one end of the pouch, making sounds of ecstasy. Wild honey was not easy to find, and not easy to take in this part of the forest. The bees' nests were high, and usually on the biggest of the trees. This nest had been more accessible, although Tomme had three small stings for his trouble.

Wanadi was watching his youngest wife, Caya, as she strung up the game from the back rafters of their hearth space, below the wide, circular roof. Tomme saw Uluru's frown, and then realized that Pequi, with Wanadi's youngest child at her breast, was looking very disgruntled. Pequi was not having an easy time in Wanadi's hearth space, since the older woman, Uluru, was the chief's confidante, and Caya was the focus for his affection.

As Caya stepped out from the storing place, ducking as she passed through the lines of ceremonial feathers waiting to be made into costumes, Wanadi picked up the puma skin and gave it to her. He smiled at her and the girl looked delighted with the gift.

"Do you like it?" the old man asked, and Caya began to say, "It's wonderful."

But Uluru made a hissing sound and the two women exchanged a swift, angry glance. Whatever was said in that moment, it was beyond Tomme's ability to hear, or understand, or recognize. But Caya had received the message and, with her face still registering her disappointment, she turned to Pequi. She gave her elder the puma skin.

"Pequi, look what our husband has brought you."

Pequi's face brightened. She smiled hugely and reached for the skin, feeling the thick fur between her fingers and smelling the raw inside.

Wanadi shook his head. But he was amused at the way he had been told off; it was a lesson in consideration that was not lost on him. He dipped a finger in Uluru's fast-vanishing pool of honey and walked across the compound towards his brother's hearth space. He called out to the man that they should talk about the Fierce People. Tomme wanted to talk about them too, but the time for that would come when he was a man.

He looked at Mapi and at his friend Jani, and for a moment saw foolish children, boys who were irritating in their naïvety.

Then Mapi said, "We're going to the pool. Jani says he's seen the girls from Tokowaya's village swimming there."

The boys seemed foolish no longer.

The pool was deep but crystal clear, fed by a stream that tumbled over slick, grey rocks where the fishing was good. That stream wound through the forest, so narrow for most of its length that the canopy closed over it, and it was a secret river, the river of the Invisible People. There were three villages along its length—Wanadi's closest to the main river, then Tokowaya's, with Chekema's nearly a day's walk away.

There were no girls in sight, but the inviting water made up considerably for the disappointment. Mapi and Jani leapt straight in and began to dive to the pool's bottom, searching for emeralds, which was a vain but pleasurable task. Tomme stripped off his soft bark loincloth, then carefully removed the feathered armlets and anklets. He took the feathers from his hair too, intending to save them, even though he would now wear more formal and brilliant "plumage."

Naked, still heavily covered with green paint, he jumped into the cool water and dived deep. The paint stayed on his body for a few minutes, then washed off in great colorful swirls. The surface of the pool shimmered emerald green for a while, before the slow flow of water carried the forest dye away.

Suddenly Jani hissed his friends into silence. They trod water, then swam to the shallows, lying belly-flat and listening.

"I *told* you!" Jani said. Beyond the rocks they could hear an almost surreptitious splashing, the cautious approach of two or three people. Tomme crawled through the shallows, hauling himself forward using the paku-weed fronds, and gripping the wet rocks. Beyond the small rapids the stream was wider, and waist-deep in its middle.

Three girls were slowly wading through the water. Each carried a small snakewood bow, decorated with purple and red feathers at each end. Arrows with bone points were nocked and ready to shoot if one of the girls spied a fish.

For a moment they were unaware of the bright, interested eyes that watched them from the rocks, then one of them saw Tomme's blond hair and all three girls straightened up, tossing their long, rich black hair back over their shoulders.

They stared at the boys from Wanadi's village.

Tomme was dumbstruck. The thoughts in his head, and the feelings in his body, were new to him; they were anxiety, he knew that; and they were excitement, he knew that too. But the sight of the tallest of the girls had set every muscle in his body vibrating wildly. His thoughts were like night birds, confused, fast, hard to grasp.

"Who *is* that girl . . . ?" he finally whispered.

Next to him, Mapi cast his friend an inquisitive glance. "That's

Kachiri. That's Tokowaya's youngest daughter."

"Kachiri?" Tomme repeated, frowning as he thought of the last time he had seen this girl. It had been two hunt-trails ago. They had all been swimming in this very stream, and the children from Wanadi's village had made mock war upon the children from upriver. It had been a grand day, and Tomme had hardly remarked the girl. Now that he stared at her, now that he studied her carefully, he could see that her features were the same. And yet . . .

And yet this was a different girl. This was an adult. Her body was so full, now, and the water glistening on her copper skin made her seem to radiate warmth and love. She was shaking slightly. Her eyes were glinting—dark eyes, wide as they watched the boys.

And they were watching Tomme in particular.

Tomme noticed everything about her, everything above the waist at least. Her lips seemed to be speaking to him. Her wide nostrils were smelling his forest scent; her eyes were feasting on him, as his feasted upon her. In every quick motion she was calling to him, the way she pushed back her hair, the way she cocked her head, the way she never smiled. She let the arrow tip trail in the water before her, so that a ripple in the current encompassed her hips, like Tomme's arms might soon encompass her whole body.

Yes, he thought. Kachiri. Tomme. If she'll have me, then Wanadi's son will marry Tokowaya's youngest daughter. Just as soon as I am a man . . .

The spell broke. Jani was giggling, sharing a joke with his brother. The girls, too, were laughing now. Kachiri called out loudly, "So Wanadi's boy is all grown up. Or is he? Slithering about like a fish on his belly, it's hard to tell."

It was a delicious taunt. Tomme grinned and slid forward, off the rocks and into the deeper stream. Mapi came with him. Tomme said loudly to his friend, "Do you want the tall one? The way she holds that bow, I don't think she knows how to hold a man . . ."

Mapi said, "No, you can have her. But make sure you have plenty of other wives."

Kachiri said to her friends, quite audibly, "He'll need several wives to make sure he's got one that doesn't mind a fish-belly in the hammock."

There was again much laughter. And yet, still the eyes of the girl, and Tomme's own startled, bright blue stare were intertwined. The two of them taunted and teased each other, and each of them knew why, and their friends did too, joining in with the fun.

Kachiri affected displeasure and impatience. "Hush, you boys. Can't you see we're fishing? This is village work. We haven't time to play games."

Still floating in the water, using a gentle breast-stroke to maintain his position, Tomme swam a little further forward, now, coming to within ten paces of the girls.

"You're not going to shoot a fish," he said, "a fish is going to shoot you—"

He snaked his arm towards her under the water's surface. Mapi laughed loudly, enjoying the suggestive joke. Kachiri's friends stepped back a little, their bows relaxed, their round faces solemn. Kachiri herself looked puzzled for a moment. Then she looked down at the water, jumped and squealed, as if something had touched her in a sensitive place.

Tomme imagined that the girl was playing along with his advance. Kachiri squealed again, and splashed at the river by her waist. Tomme looked round, where he floated, and grinned at Mapi and Jani, who were looking on, astonished. They had seen Wanadi perform strange tricks, but had no idea that his son could do the same.

A moment later the reason for Kachiri's squealing became apparent. She screamed, "Piranha! Piranha!"

Tomme yelled at the top of his voice, suddenly shocked, all thought of love and teasing gone. He stood up and splashed noisily to the river bank, holding his hands over his genitals even after they were dangling safely above the stream. Beside him, Mapi and Jani too were running in fright, reaching safety as they shrieked their panic.

On the shore they stopped and turned to see where the girls had gone.

They were still in the river, and laughing hysterically. Kachiri was so amused at her joke that she fell over backwards. Her friends helped her back to her feet, grabbing for her bow before it floated away.

Tomme removed his hands from their protective position and made fish-like swimming motions towards the girl. Kachiri stopped laughing and stared at Tomme for a long, appraising moment. Then she smiled quickly, cocked her head, and turned back up-stream, walking towards her village. Her friends followed her, murmuring quietly together, and casting quick glances back at the boys on the bank.

5

Crouched on his haunches at the edge of the forest, Wanadi watched the whole incident in the stream. If he smiled, as he saw the taunting relationship between Tomme and Kachiri, it was with pride: pride that his son from the wilderness should now, quite clearly, be confronting the time of change; and pride, too, that Tomme should have demonstrated such an eye for beauty, because Kachiri was luscious and ripe, like the most magnificent of fruits, and she was strong, too, strong in spirit and in limb. And if Wanadi frowned, the frown was one of sadness, because it was Tomme's time to die, and after the hunt-death he would no longer be Wanadi's special child, the white child, the ghost child . . .

As he watched the youngsters at play, he found himself longing for the moment to extend forever. He would crouch here for ever and watch the vitality, and the fun, and the innocence of the children who faced each other in the water that he called Little Snake Water. What a lovely way to go into the spirit-world, he thought. If my last memory could be such a one as this, an image of pleasure, and young love, and passion . . . how strong I would be in the dream-light realm.

Tomme taunted Kachiri and the lithe and graceful young woman answered back, blow for blow, arrow for arrow. She was magnificent. She was more beautiful than his own young wife, Caya. Her breasts were like copper-colored fruits. When Wanadi had been Tomme's age he had not been interested in anything save eyes, mouth and running speed. With the passing of the seasons young flesh appealed to him in different ways.

He smiled as he thought of this. Even after the time of change, men—women too, he imagined—continued to go through changes. Like a snake shedding its skin not once but many times. Like the wasps and bees that continually moved to different parts of the forest, outgrowing their need for one place, finding other flower fields below the canopy, other nesting sites.

Kachiri . . . Kachiri . . . how inviting her face was, how sensitive her fingers looked. Wanadi sighed and shuffled restlessly where he crouched, imagining the sweet young one tussling with him in the hammock. He was repressing a thought. The thought was that if Tomme *did* bond with the girl then he, Wanadi, would have the right to hammock with the girl. But he knew that he couldn't do that. In times past, perhaps. But times changed.

If Kachiri shared Tomme's hearth, there would be a bond between Wanadi's people and those of Tokowaya. That would be good. It would mean a dowry of pigs and poison, for a start, probably enough for a full rainy season. It would also mean more of the exquisitely fashioned blow-pipes that Tokowaya's people made from bamboo. They knew a way of burning the insides to make them straighter and truer than anything Wanadi could produce. They would never reveal their secret, but they would trade in these conventionally untradable items if Kachiri and Tomme were bonded.

Good. Things were looking up. What else?

Only one thing chilled Wanadi's spirit. Tomme was a ghost. He was from the wilderness, beyond the edge of the World. And he was not yet a man, he had not died. Maybe Tokowaya would forbid the union. Maybe that old, crotchety chieftain would decide that Kachiri was worth the bond of one of Chekema's scrawny roosters. Chekema! Wanadi silently spat as he thought of that arrogant hunter-chief. To think that they had had the same ancestors. They had drunk the same powdered bones. The same ghosts lived in their hearts and loins.

There was only one thing to do, Wanadi decided. Tomme *had* to marry Kachiri, because a liaison with Chekema's people at this time would not cause the same pleasant breezes to blow through the great forest. But to achieve this end, first Tomme had to die. And then he had to be instructed carefully on how to court the girl . . .

And he had to be told the unpleasant truth: that as a ghost, even as a man–ghost, if Tokowaya was not prepared to release his daughter to Tomme son-of-Wanadi, Tomme would be killed the first moment he entered Tokowaya's village. A real death. The death of the flesh.

And not even his spirit to remain in the ash of his father's fire.

The thought induced in Wanadi a terrible panic which belied his calm, smiling exterior. He realized how much this ghost boy, sent to him from the wilderness by the Great Anaconda to replace his own dead son, how much Tomme had come to represent all that the old man lived for. He acknowledged how much he needed to see Tomme in command in the village. He let himself recognize his hope that before he died he would listen to Tomme's stories, the stories of the man, hunt stories, and stories of war, and most particularly, the stories of Tomme's ghostlight, the dead forests, the strange peoples, the sinister visions that he remembered from his time in the wilderness.

Uluru was suddenly beside him. She dropped to a crouch beside her husband and watched Tomme swimming towards the beautiful Kachiri. Uluru was without her child and she put an arm around Wanadi's broad shoulder.

"What are you looking at? You've seen Tomme play before."

"Not like this," Wanadi said. Again he sighed. He felt the old woman's tension, her sudden caught breath. But when he glanced at her she was smiling, staring straight ahead, as if nothing had worried her.

Strong. Strong like Kachiri would be strong. Strong like his own mother had been. When she had been young, Uluru had been wanted by many chieftain's sons, and Wanadi had pursued her and won her love, and her bond, only after a great personal struggle. She was the wisest person he knew. Her word, her advice, was everything that made him the great chief he was . . . except, of course, that he was a magnificent hunter. That was all his *own* doing.

He felt for her now, recognizing what she must be feeling. Perhaps the lesson of his insensitivity a while earlier had sharpened his awareness of the sadness of others.

He put his arm round her and hugged her. She rested a hand on his knee, touched her head to his.

"Must it be? He's still so young."

"He's not young at all," Wanadi said. "He came from the wilderness. Perhaps he was older than we thought. In any case, the time has come. The time for him to die."

Uluru's body shuddered, and tears ran down her cheeks. "I would like to hold Tomme one last time."

Wanadi glanced at her. "So would I," he said. "But for me, such things are gone."

Suddenly the boys were running from the river. Kachiri's cry of "Piranha! Piranha!" fooled Wanadi for a moment, until he saw how the girls remained in the stream, laughing at the scampering male forms in front of them.

As Tomme stood on the river shore, brazenly gesturing to the girl, Wanadi and Uluru approached him. He seemed startled when Wanadi addressed him, and looked a little shamefaced.

Wanadi said sternly, "So. This is Tomme. He fights the Fierce People with his father. He hunts well. He speaks like a man to the girls from the village of Tokowaya. But he runs from their taunting like a little boy."

Tomme flushed red below his tanned skin. He met his father's gaze evenly, bravely. "I'm sorry," he said. "I should not have run."

"A man would not have run," Wanadi said stiffly. Tomme watched him, waiting. He looked nervous. He glanced at his mother. Wanadi said softly, "Tomme, the time has come for you to die."

With that the old chief turned away from the boy, calling to two of the men of the village. Tomme's heart was beating fast. He wanted to shout his joy, but he controlled the emotion. Mapi was watching him as if he had lost a dear friend, full of sadness, full of melancholy.

Uluru took Tomme in her arms and nestled him to her breast. Tomme resisted for a moment, not wanting his friends to see this show of affection. Then something in him melted. He hugged his mother, and the hug grew stronger, and in a moment or two both of them were crying softly.

"Goodbye, Tomme," Uluru whispered. "Goodbye, my ghost son."

6

By night they led him into the forest, surrounding him with the light of torches as they made their way to the place of dying. The shadows of the forest loomed large around him, and Tomme felt frightened, even though he was with the men of the village. Cats growled and birds flew noisily above them, disturbed from their rest in the high canopy. The fire from the torches set light to the dry liana, which flared briefly, thin streamers of fire reaching up into the dark void of the heavens.

An Old One had been heard in the jungle, and Tomme would have to face it. As yet he had no idea of the nature of the jaws that would close around him. The warriors knew, though, and because they shared this terrible secret they walked in silence, and Tomme felt alone among the men.

He was quite naked, not even a feather in his hair. He was decorated, though, and his father and mother had painted the symbols and the marks of protection upon him themselves. Winding round his body was the green line of the Great Anaconda. Flecks of white were the symbols of his bones, which would one day be burned and drunk by the people of the village, and then returned to the forest. On his arms were the leaf-patterns that recollected the time, in the dreamlight, when all the people had been in the form of great trees. On his legs were the grey stone-shapes that symbolized the time before the trees, when all of life had been in the rocks. Finally, on his back was the red and yellow of the fire that would one day burn him. Mixed with the paint was his own blood, drawn from the deep cuts that Wanadi had inflicted in his flesh: blood and fire, but behind him, still, and pushing him forward to manhood, and to life.

Soon they reached the wide green spread of a pool, its surface thick with weed and scum. The smell of it was strong, the smell of rot, of stagnation. This was a terrible place. There were no animal tracks leading to it. Even the trees were stunted and twisted, reaching out over the still water and trembling slightly, as if they feared what would break the surface . . .

Watching, Tomme shuddered as the green surface rippled and a long, slender shape slid towards the near bank. It was an anaconda, probably more than four man-lengths long. It watched the fire of the torches, then turned and could be seen swimming across the pool by the way the dense weed shifted.

"You must stand here," Wanadi said, "and face it."

"Face what, father?" Tomme whispered. He was still watching the place where the snake was lurking. He dreaded the thought of what it could do to him.

Around him the men backed away, lowering their torches in front of them so that Tomme felt himself surrounded by a ring of fire, the shapes of the warriors lost in the darkness behind. Wanadi walked about him three times, then turned and repeated the action. He stood before his son and touched an eagle's feather to the boy's eyes and lips, then traced a pattern on his body.

All the time that he did this he whispered the calling words, and the words of protection. Tomme tried to understand them, but he could hear unpleasant, frightening sounds from the jungle behind him, and unnerving splashings from the stagnant forest pool in front of him.

"An Old One is coming, a Great One. The time is right. The Great One is coming for the boy Tomme. It will take the boy in its jaws and swallow him. The Great One is like a river, like a Great Snake . . ."

Shaking like a leaf, Tomme watched his father. Their bodies gleamed in the torchlight. The dark shapes of the trees crowded closer to them, reaching to them, rustling and whispering . . .

Wanadi reached out to his son and forcibly turned the boy away from the pool. He faced the darkness of the forest, now, and his eyes widened with dread as he heard the moaning and movement of the Great One who was approaching him.

Not the anaconda, then. Not the snake . . .

Something worse, something far worse!

His body became icily cold as he stood his ground. His mind filled with ghostly images, strange memories, word memories from his time in the wilderness . . .

A girl with white skin, reaching for an ant, her face beaming with pleasure, innocent pleasure. She seemed to be saying, ants are nice. He shuddered at the sight of the way she played with the vicious insect.

I don't like them. I can't stand them. Not insects, not ants . . . not ants . . .

He felt dizzy with the memories, confused by this echo of ancient fear. He had a dread of spiders, and of crawling things, although he had grown used to them; they were such a familiar sight to him now. But he would not have sought the company of the tiny forest life that scuttled and marched in the microcosm . . .

Marching . . . marching . . . a column of creatures, an endless, crawling trail of them, coming towards him, consuming and stripping the life of the forest in its path.

The torchlit jungle ahead of him began to glisten darkly, as if a dark liquid were slowly oozing over the vegetation. The branches of the trees shook, the leaves rattled like bones. The dark stain came closer and began to ascend Tomme's body. It ran and crawled across his skin, a thick layer of ants that searched and scurried across his face, his hair, his back. By the pool the column of insects spread out and sought a way across. They rose up the trees and crawled across the branches. The green pool became black. The surface quivered and pulsed as the carpet of ants moved inexorably forward.

The haunting notes of four bone flutes filled the night air; brief pulses of sound, becoming more and more frantic, they seemed to reflect the rapid beating of Tomme's heart, and the way his spirit became more and more agitated as the ants completely smothered him. He trembled and tried to scream, but as ants poured into his mouth he slammed his jaws shut. His arms were raised from his sides. He was a seething black shape by the shore of the pond, and the deeper sound of bamboo pipes now cut across the shriller sounds of the bone.

Wanadi watched his son. "It has taken the boy into its jaws," he said loudly. "It seeks out the true heart of the boy."

Tomme remained standing for five minutes. The flutes played, the forest waited. Out on the pond something thrashed below the dark, creeping surface, a great green tail rose above the ants and the slime and vanished again.

Tomme sank to his knees. His arms fell to his sides. He toppled over, turning as he fell, so that he watched the canopy through the thin slits of his swollen eyelids.

Wanadi made a quick gesture and the music stopped. The warriors stared at the motionless boy by the flickering light of the dying torches. Tomme's father said, "The boy is dead. Tomme is dead." And as he said the words the hunters of the Invisible People knelt and remained in silence.

Soon the column of ants moved on. It seemed that they passed across the clearing and the pool and the trees above the pool for most of the night. Eventually the rattling of the foliage and the restless murmur of their passage ceased. The pool became green again. The forest seemed to become alive again.

Wanadi rose to his feet, went over to Tomme's body. A few ants were crawling on his skin and in his hair. Wanadi crouched down and brushed them away.

"The boy is dead," he whispered sadly.

Tomme opened his eyes. He sucked in his breath sharply, then spat, then coughed. He moaned a little and began to flex his arms. He closed his eyes again against the pain.

Wanadi said, "The man is born. Welcome to life, Tomme. Welcome to the world."

"Tell me what you saw when you were dead," Wanadi murmured as he smeared soothing ointment on to Tomme's swollen, bitten body. Tomme was shivering, a fever developing from the ant attack. His flesh was red and raw, his lips and eyes puffy, but he was smiling. He lay in Wanadi's hammock, close to the fire, and let himself be nursed for these few hours.

"I saw strange sights," Tomme said, and winced as the ointment stung a particularly deep bite.

He didn't care. He had died and he had been born again. He had survived being eaten by the Great One. He had triumphed over his hunt-death.

"Tell me about your ghost father," Wanadi said gently. He met Tomme's red-eyed gaze evenly as the young man started with surprise. Then Tomme realized that he could hide nothing from his father.

"Yes," he whispered. "Yes, I saw my ghost father again. It was very real. He is a man unlike any man in the village. He has dark hair but very white skin, and wears purple cloth all round his body. I saw him with the Termite People, with their yellow tree-eaters. I saw him running . . ."

Tomme strained to sit up, frowning slightly. "He was running towards the World. He was shouting but I couldn't hear any sound. He was waving his arm, and the more he ran the further away he seemed to go, as if the World were running away from *him*."

He lay back again. "I felt very sad for him. Why was he running?"

Wanadi smoothed ointment on to Tomme's face, and in the same motion soothed the hot skin. "Did you see your ancestors?" he asked.

"I don't know. There were people, many people. They all wore the clothes that cover the body . . ."

"Termite People," Wanadi agreed. "They always feel the cold."

"They were walking along wide tracks. The land around them was strange—dead—the trees were stunted, the huts were white and cold. And I saw shining pools with pictures in them. One of the pictures was a man. *Charlie* . . ."

"Charlie?'

"That was his name. He had the way of changing things without touching them, calling without speaking . . . that's all I remember . . ."

Wanadi was interested by that. He glanced at Uluru, sitting close by. "Such people used to exist," he said. "Not like us. They lived in the dreamlight. Sometimes one is born who can call the forest, and the creatures of the forest."

He looked at Tomme. "Creatures like the eagles, or the great cats . . ."

After a moment's hesitation, Tomme said, "I called an eagle once . . ."

"I know," Wanadi said, smiling slightly. "You've called other things as well."

"Other things?"

"Little things. Unimportant things. A long time ago, when you were still in the wilderness, you called to me."

"To you?" Tomme stared at his father as Wanadi daubed the cleansing and soothing vegetable grease upon the young man's blistered skin.

Wanadi sat back on his haunches and frowned, staring into the hearth. "Perhaps it was me who called to you. I can't remember now." Again he met the bright blue gaze of his son. "It doesn't matter. The Light of the Forest guided us together, that's all that matters. And now you are a man, and you will have a hearth of your own . . ." Wanadi grinned and winked as Tomme struggled to raise himself on to his elbows. "And maybe a certain ripe young flower from the village of Tokowaya . . ."

"Kachiri," Tomme breathed, and a very different light shone in his pale, strange eyes.

7

Tomme was given his own hearth, now, and with that came the expectation that he would find himself a partner. Samanpo's daughter was disappointed when Tomme let it be known that his interest lay in the village of Tokowaya. But she placed half of a broken reed whistle on his hearth, while he still lay recovering from his ordeal in Wanadi's hammock, and kept the other half for herself. This was as clear a sign as any that she would like to be Tomme's second wife.

After a day sleeping, Tomme stood and walked alone to the dark space below the palm thatch where a small fire had been laid ready for him to light. From each family round the shabano there was a gift of fruit and food, but better gifts were to come. Mapi watched his friend from the middle of the enclosure, then left Jani and ran over to Tomme, falling into step beside him. Round the village the fires were burning, and in the middle space the ceremonial fire was being lit.

Tonight would be a time for talking, and a time for visiting the dreamlight.

Mapi watched his friend carefully, disturbed at the way Tomme ignored him. "What did they do to you? Was it really ants? Did it hurt?"

Tomme glanced at him disdainfully, then stepped to his hearth and crouched down. He picked up the small fire sticks, toyed with them, then positioned them to start the flame.

Mapi watched him, shuffling from foot to foot and glancing apprehensively at his brother. To Tomme, he said, "Is it a secret? Is that why you're not talking?"

Without looking at him, Tomme said, "Go away, Mapi."

He began to grind the sticks together. Smoke came, then fire, and he blew the fire on to dry straw, which he pushed below the cut wood. Soon his fire was burning well, and by its sparse light Mapi's face glistened with tears. The boy turned away, back to the other children. After a hunt-trail, maybe two, he too would undergo his hunt-death. He would have his own hearth, and he and Tomme would be friends again. Until then . . .

As he walked away from the new fire he didn't notice Tomme's pained and sad glance after him.

It was a time of celebration. The shabano glowed with light and fire, filled with the smell of roasting pig, vibrated to the sound of log drums and the music of bone and bamboo flutes. Tomme sat by his fire. He had invited his parents to sit with him, and Caya and Pequi too, dressed in their ceremonial colors, sat in Tomme's hearth space. Each family brought him a gift. He received spears, and a snakewood bow, and two sheaths stuffed with the long, barbed arrows of the village. He was given a flute, a stone axe, sheets of soft bark, bundles of richly colored feathers, and whole strings of bone, stone and wood decorative clothing.

Wanadi himself gave Tomme a head-dress. Tomme hadn't seen it being made. It fitted tightly round the cropped thatch of his hair and hung to his knees. It had a crest of macaw and toucan feathers, borders of finch and bluebird tail feathers and even the wing feathers of the small red bird that was known as the "tear of the forest," the *jarakit*.

Best of all, though, on the part of the head-dress that would rest upon his shoulders were the magnificent spread wing feathers of the gold-breasted eagle. Almost as long as Tomme's arm, these feathers formed shoulder plumes that seemed to move like wings as he raised and lowered his arms. They were striking feathers, slightly curved, black-tipped and gold-veined, and white where the feather blade was widest.

From this dress he plucked a small blue feather and worked it into the tip, below the stone blade, of his ceremonial spear.

"My first hunt," he said. "But watch out, monkeys! Soon I'm going to want a cloak of ringtails and a loincloth of howler fur . . ."

The forest around the village seemed to shift a little in the glimmering, eerie light from below.

Later, the men gathered round the central fire and Wanadi brought the clay pot containing *cocassa* to the circle. Cocassa was a dry, green powder, ground very finely. It came from the seeds of a plant that grew many days' walking to the north. Only a few men in the village knew how to prepare it, and how to say the words of the dreamlight. In his time Tomme might be lucky, and be chosen. To be the best hunter, the best warrior, even the chief of the village—these did not necessarily guarantee that a man would share the secret of the dreamlight.

A small amount of the powder was placed in the tip of a narrow cane tube. This was held horizontally and passed around the circle, each man calling upon his animal guide to take him safely on his journey into the other realm, the place where their ancestors still lived.

When Tomme received the pipe he held it between his eyes and the fire and spoke the words he had been told. He called upon the Old Ones to find him a suitable and courageous animal guide for his spirit-trip. He recounted the manner of his death and rebirth. He pledged his courage in the hunt, and his sureness with bow, spear and blow-pipe. He promised to honor each and every creature that he killed.

Samanpo would be the first to voyage into the dreamlight. His youngest child had been taken by a jaguar four days before. Now he would voyage into the other world and seek the child's spirit, bringing it safely back to the hearth. Samanpo's animal guide was a howler, a great male monkey that growled and spat, and moved through the canopy with the speed of an arrow.

He knelt before Wanadi, who placed one end of the cane tube in his brother's nostril, then quickly blew the green powder into the man's body. The effect on Samanpo was almost instantaneous. He howled, he screamed, and then he danced. The drums picked up the rhythm of his movements, beating him through his journey, racing with him as he flung himself from branch to branch, hesitating warily as he sought among the spirits for his child . . .

Tomme waited, excitedly, impatiently. All his friends talked about the dreamlight, and what it must be like . . . and now he would find out for himself. At last. He had chewed the roots, and drunk the dark, pungent liquids which could give wild, wonderful dreams. But they were not the same, they were for fun, and for getting rid of pain . . .

Like the pain of his memories. Like the pain of his sadness. When he had first lived among the Invisible People he had been frightened and lost, and terribly lonely. Uluru, his mother, had helped ease that pain, and he had chewed the strange white roots and drifted into spinning, dizzy dreams. Each hunt-trail, as he grew older, each *year* as he would have said in his old language, he forgot a little more.

With forgetting came peace. A wonderful peace. Such a peace that now there was no sadness in him at all, and the few words and images from his old life which he had carried through the ten hunt-trails were precious fragments of a world as otherly and unreal as the spirit-world to which he would now voyage . . .

Wanadi turned to him, and raised the cane pipe. Cocassa dust shimmered green in its bore; Tommy reached for it, and held the pipe into his nostril, closing his eyes as he listened for Wanadi's quick breath.

When the drug entered his body it was as if he had been struck a violent yet painless blow. He recoiled, shouting out with shock. A moment later his body felt as light as air, and he seemed to be floating above the compound, arms outstretched. The fires swirled before his eyes, becoming dizzying circles of brightness. The trees stretched above him, and then shrank away below. The earth toppled and spun. The men round the fire, smiling as they watched him, dropped away, appearing as tiny shapes grouped around the tiny glow of the flames.

The Light of the World changed from night's darkness to an eerie green, in which the land stretched away, and the distant mountains glistened with the snow on their high peaks.

The wind took him. He felt its gentle fingers carry his body higher. He sailed rapidly across the great forest, and the wind tugged him down, then pushed him to the right, and he whirled and wheeled and . . .

. . . reached out his wings. Struck hard against the air, felt his body soar, struck again and turned to watch the canopy below. He feathered and fell, beat his wings hard again and leveled off, skimming the tree tops, circling the clearing where the fires of Wanadi's village were bright points of light in the green . . .

He flew to the east, striking hard, riding the high winds with astonishing ease. Soon he could see the edge of the World, where the forest ended and the great waste land began. There, too, there were lights, and he circled high above them, and saw the river below, and the great rock wall that had been built across it.

In the dreamlight, as in the real world, all things existed, but it was their spirit presence that he witnessed from his free-flying form, now, and as such there was little to be seen, since the spirits were so tiny in the wilderness.

Back across the forest. Back into the dreamlight of the World. Below him he could see all the fires of all the times, the forest opening its canopy to let him glimpse where, in the past, there had been villages, and hunt-trails. The Old Ones watched him, and the Great Ones, and he saw the Great Anaconda, sliding through the forest, gouging the great trough in which the rivers would flow.

Below him, crystal waters tumbled and roared across grey rocks, and in their dreamlight depths, a deeper, more vibrant green glittered and beckoned to him. He swooped low. The lights were like fire, below the water's surface. They seemed to dance and play like fish, but they were stones, bright green stones.

They were the Lights of the Forest. They had shown themselves to the eagle. They had shown themselves to Tomme . . .

The sensation of wind, and of being high above the earth, and of soaring over woodland—all these faded suddenly away, and Tomme opened his eyes. It was dark night again, with the yellow, dancing figures of flames, and the flickering shadows of the Invisible People all around him, watching him.

He was on his back and he struggled to sit up, shaking his head to clear his thoughts. He could hardly speak. He seemed to have no strength in his limbs. Wanadi was crouched before him, looking excitedly at Tomme's face, perhaps trying to read there some indication of what his son had seen.

"It's true," the old man whispered. He was smiling. "My son *is* an eagle. You are the eagle-caller, Tomme. You came to us from the wilderness. We were called to the edge of the World to find you. There is a great purpose here, a great reason . . ."

He seemed expectant, waiting, watching Tomme as if Tomme, now, would reveal some great truth.

All Tomme could remember was the waste land, and the green fire in the water.

"Green fire . . ." he murmured, his speech slurred and difficult. "I saw it. Green fire . . . in the waterfall."

Wanadi's eyes widened, his lips parted. He emitted a sound that was both shock and wonderment. "The Light of the Forest! You have seen the Light of the Forest!"

"It was to the east, beyond the first river. It was in the place where the Fierce People live."

Wanadi came closer. "That place is where our own people used to live. It is the only place we know where the Light of the Forest can be found. When the Fierce People came, with their appetite for our flesh, we fled across the rivers, deeper into the forest. That was many generations ago, before my life, before my great-grandfather's life. We have not dared to go back to that place . . ."

Tomme said, "The Light of the Forest is there. I shall fetch it. I shall hunt for it. Then Kachiri will come to my hearth."

Wanadi smiled. "Brave words, Tomme." He helped Tomme to sit up, then drew a small pouch from his loincloth. The pouch, made of puma skin, rattled as he opened it. On to the ground he spilled five emeralds, five small green stones.

"This is all that is left of our Light, Tomme. In these stones is the Light that gives power to our paint, that makes us the Invisible People. When these are gone, and with each chief who dies one of them is returned to the dreamlight, when they are gone, we shall no longer be the Invisible People. The forest will shrink away from us, and leave us naked to the teeth and jaws of the Termite People."

Tomme picked up the stones and cradled them in his hands.

"I shall never let that happen. The eagle has shown me where to find the Light of the Forest. And I am a man, now, and I choose the nature of my hunt-trails. This shall be my first."

Wanadi settled back upon his haunches and smiled at his son. But behind the smile, behind his narrowed eyes, there was a look that, if Tomme had been able to see it, he would have recognized as anguish.

8

Kachiri was picking fruit with her cousins, close to the river's edge, between her village and that of Wanadi. It was early morning and a fine steam rose from the forest floor, brilliantly illuminated by the sunlight which broke through the thin canopy. There was a hush about the forest, and the furtive movement in the bushes close to her was immediately obvious.

For a moment she was inclined to step away from where the animal, or human, was hiding. Her first instinct said *cat*. Her second, *Fierce People*. But her third thought, and the one she favored, was of an altogether different watcher.

She hummed to herself, and stepped closer to the magnolia. She reached for one of the brilliant blossoms, and a hand snaked out and grabbed her wrist, tugging her out of sight of her cousins.

She was deeply shocked as she saw the young man crouching there, his eyes so intense, his breathing so ragged. He was painted totally in green. He had a large black feather stuck in his hair, and across his crown. Flowers garlanded his neck and waist. His penis was tied against his belly, signifying that he was going to make a long run through the wood. Behind him, on the floor of the forest, were his weapons, and they were the weapons of a man, and of a warrior.

She might not have recognized Tomme but for his blue eyes.

"I need you," he said. "And you need me. I want you to share my hearth, and my hammock."

Kachiri tugged away from him, frightened by his earnest presence, intrigued by his obvious warrior status . . . liking the feeling of love and desire which he radiated from behind the mask.

"Why have you dressed like a man . . . ?"

"Because I *am* a man. I have undergone my hunt-death."

Kachiri shivered slightly. He was of age, then. And so was she. Perhaps his father had seen the need for adulthood in his son just as her mother had seen that need in her. Without knowing it, then, they had passed from childhood together, perhaps during the same long night. Perhaps the sparks from the fires of their village had mingled in the night sky . . .

She looked at him and she loved him. His bearing was proud and his body was like a jaguar's, lean and supple. He looked strong, he made *her* feel strong, and she could see that he was responding to her own strength of spirit . . . and to her beauty. There was a fire burning inside his chest that made her own heart miss its rhythm. She would bond with the ghost warrior. She wanted it more than anything. He was from beyond the World, but he was a man in all but color. She would have him as her husband. But it would be done properly.

She taunted him still. "So you're a man. And now you have become a man you say everything that other men say to me. Why should I listen to you rather than them?"

Her cousins were calling to her, alarmed at her sudden disappearance.

Engineer Bill Markham (Powers Boothe) shows his son Tommy (William Rodriguez) and daughter Heather (Yara Vaneau) around the construction site of the dam he is building.

Young Tommy (William Rodriguez) strays into the jungle during a family picnic at the damsite.

Tommy (Charley Boorman), now grown up and known as "Tomme," on a hunting expedition with his 'new' father, Chief Wanadi of the "Invisible People" (Rui Polonah).

Tomme prepares to strike Kachiri (Dira Paes) during the ritualized wedding ceremony.

Tomme kneels over his dying spiritual father, Chief Wanadi; and realizes he must now carry on as leader of the "Invisible People."

All photographs courtesy of Embassy Films

Tomme awaits the ordeal of his manhood ceremony, in which he must withstand an onslaught of ants.

Bill Markham arranges a selection of gifts to attract the Indians who he hopes will lead him to his lost son.

Bill Markham confronts the "Fierce People" during his search for his son.

Director John Boorman with his son Charley during filming of The Emerald Forest.

Tomme stepped forward. He touched her gently on the shoulders. "I am more than other men. I am going on my first hunt alone, but I'm not hunting animals."

She frowned. "What then?"

"I'm going to bring back the Light of the Forest." He straightened up as he spoke. He looked haughty, proud. Kachiri watched him and knew that he meant every word. His appearance may have been conceited, now, but there was a great dignity in that conceit.

The Light of the Forest? She knew well enough what that meant, and where it entailed traveling.

"The Fierce People will catch you!" she said.

"They won't see me," Tomme retorted, grinning.

"They *will*. They'll cook you and eat you, the whole tribe of them, even the grandfathers without teeth."

He laughed at her. She glared at him as he backed away. He stooped and picked up his arrows and spears, then uttered a call like a small bird. With a final salute he stepped into the tangled growth of the forest and was suddenly invisible to her. Kachiri stepped forward and listened and looked. She parted the leaves where Tomme had vanished but saw nothing.

Puzzled, she turned away. She cocked her head and listened hard, but he was travelling away from her without the slightest sound.

Except that, as she stepped back into the slight clearing where her cousins were waiting for her, the same small bird trilled, almost directly in her ear.

She gasped and swung round.

There was no bird to be seen.

By dusk he had reached the river where he and Wanadi had turned back the Fierce People. He was exhausted but happy. He had made good ground on this, his first solitary hunt-trail. Once, he knew, he had been made to run all the way from the edge of the World. Part of that terrifying journey remained in his mind. Sometimes Wanadi had carried him. A lot of the time, all the hunting band had used narrow, flimsy boats, and paddled themselves against the current, deeper into the rainforest. Most of the time he had run, and the days had passed, and then the weeks, and later he had forgotten how to measure time in anything more than nights . . .

The edge of the World was now fourteen nights away, by forest, by river and by hidden track. Then, so long ago, the edge of the World had been nearly twice as far.

He drank at the river's edge, and suddenly realized that a sleek, young jaguar was drinking on the far bank. Man and animal saw each other at the same time; yellow eyes met blue, and each side growled.

Tomme reached slowly for his bow, not breaking the stare. "Look out, my friend," he said softly, but audibly. "Next time you and I meet I will have a wife, and if she asks me for a skin . . ."

The jaguar turned suddenly and bolted into the gloom of the jungle. Tomme smiled and stood. As Wanadi had done, that time before, he flung the corpse of a small howler monkey into the river, up-stream of the place where he now stood. As the animal drifted by he watched it. Nothing happened.

Confidently he crossed the water, and entered the darkening forest.

At night, as he slept in the warm dry places close to the big trees, he re-experienced the flight of the eagle. He could see the waterfall, where the Light of the Forest shone, as clearly as if he stood there now; and instinctively he knew that he was heading towards that place.

He could hardly wait for dawn. He was now deep into the territory where the Fierce People hunted; once, this very forest had belonged to the Invisible People. Tomme imagined that, if he looked closely, he might see the rain-rotted remnants of the old totems and villages. Of course, all he saw was the jungle.

But he ran carefully, now. He was three days from his own village. He was in a part of the rainforest where the hunters of his tribe were forbidden to go, and to which they had not ventured for generations. To go to the edge of the World was to take a hunt-trail further north. This forest was forgotten land, and it seemed to watch him, and to whisper that it knew him . . .

Undaunted, Tomme kept the green paint, with its sprinkling of emerald dust, thick and firm upon his body. He carried a gourd of the paint. Each dawn he patterned himself anew with the symbols and calling-signs of the forest, and with the secret signs that would render him invisible.

In this way he journeyed four days from the village of his father. He went deeper into danger than any other hunter of his tribe.

And early on that fourth day he heard drums, and the sound of a hunt in progress.

And the sound of water . . .

He had found the place! Attentive to the distant, fading sounds of the hunt, he ran through the forest, and emerged from the tree line by the bubbling waters of a wide, cold river. Up-stream, the water cascaded from high rocks, and formed a deep, foaming pool, a pool that even from here seemed to shimmer green.

Remembering the eagle's eye, he knew at once that this was the place where the jewels lay, and he waded quickly through the water, slipping and stumbling until he had crossed the flow, and come to crouch below the waterfall itself. The green stones lay below him, and he reached in and pulled one out, a tiny crystal, rich and green and brilliant with fire. He held it up before him, staring at the World through its translucent substance.

"The Light of the World," he whispered, and he nearly cried, because he had achieved something that Wanadi, his father, had not had the courage to try. Kachiri would be his, now, and with her the sort of fame that would make him live in the stories of the hearth for generations to come. He would tell stories himself, for this journey had been a thrilling one, and a dangerous one, and would keep the village in enraptured silence for many fireside evenings.

Quickly he placed the stones in his pouch, then plucked a handful more from the deep, clear water.

This will be enough, he thought to himself proudly. If I have been here once, I can come here again. The Invisible People will never be without their Light.

He tied the pouch round his neck again, then reached for his bow, arrows and spears. But at that moment, through the roar and crash of the water from the fall, he heard the sound of someone running through the forest . . .

In fact, it was the sound of someone *falling* through the forest, breaking branches, loosening stones, yelling as he grabbed for anything to support himself. Finally, the body struck the stream with a great splash.

Tomme was instantly alert. He had an arrow nocked and ready, and he crouched low and moved out of the steam thrown up by the waterfall. He soon saw the prey, a dark shape wading through the river towards him. There was blood on the man's face, and his skin seemed pale despite the beard and grime that coated it. He was dressed in the sort of clothes that Tomme remembered from his time with the Termite People, from the wilderness.

The man struggled through the water and Tomme realized that he had not yet been seen. Behind the wilderness man, an arrow struck the water. High on the steep bank, among the leaning, crowded trees, the figures of Fierce Hunters strained to see their quarry, and flung their spears into the river below.

Tomme rose from his crouch and stepped quickly towards the stranger. The wilderness man saw him and raised his left hand, in which he held a strange black object . . .

A gun, a gun . . . the word came from the dead part of Tomme's mind . . .

The air near Tomme buzzed with sound, and a deep rattling roar came from the wilderness man. There seemed to be fire spitting from the hole in the black pipe of the gun-weapon. The roar stopped abruptly. Tomme shot off his arrow without thinking, and saw the shaft pass close to the stranger, but miss.

He nocked a second arrow and struggled through the shallow river, knowing that he had to get away from this wild man from the outside, and from the man-eating hunters who were even now slipping and sliding down the perilous embankment.

He had taken just three steps when the wilderness man's face seemed to change. Tomme slowed, his heart beating. For a moment he thought he was at the edge of the World again, and he could see clearly a man running in an eerie, slow way towards the tree line. This was that same man. And the man, running, had been calling his name, arms flapping as he struggled to cover the distance, a bizarre human bird . . .

The eyes, the mouth, the face—Tomme felt a great shock as he realized that this wilderness creature was the ghost that had haunted him since Wanadi had brought him into the world.

"Ghost father," he whispered, then shouted aloud, *"Ghost father!"*

Behind the spectre, one of the Fierce Hunters had entered the water and was rushing at the wilderness man, spear raised.

"Be careful!" Tomme yelled. He raised his bow. His ghost father turned away, hiding his head behind his arm and falling into the water. Tomme shot quickly, and the warrior spun back, the arrow deep in his chest.

Dropping to his knees, Tomme tried to drag his ghost father out of the river. The man's haunted gaze turned on him. The pale eyes narrowed, the lips moved, a silent word, a silent question.

"Come on!" Tomme urged him. "We've got to get away, there are too many of them!"

His ghost father recognized him, then. An expression of great joy spread across his battered, bloody features. His hands closed on Tomme's arms, compulsively gripping the young man's flesh.

"Tommy!" he said. *"My God, Tommy! It's you!"*

The words were strange to Tomme, although he recognized a form of his own name.

"Ghost father, no time for this. No time to talk . . ."

An arrow stung Tomme as it passed close to his arm. Spears fell in the water around them. Ghost father staggered to his feet. Still holding Tomme, he struggled through the water, following the young man who was his ghost son.

One of the Fierce People appeared ahead of them, standing on a rock. Ghost father flung his black weapon and the hunter overbalanced and slipped out of sight.

The current took them, then, and they were swept into the water up to their necks, still clutching each other, swimming with the flow, letting the river take them away to safety.

Or so they thought.

Seconds after they had begun to swim, the river ahead of them abruptly vanished. Tomme knew immediately what that meant: a second fall. He struck hard for the rocks at the bank, half dragging the wilderness man with him. They hauled themselves to safety, and crouched, shivering, just a few feet from the sudden drop. Beyond the falls, the river wound away into a tunnel of crowded trees; it looked safe, it looked inviting . . .

Behind them, the forest crashed as the hunters came in pursuit. An arrow hummed through the air. Tomme turned quickly and drew his own bow, shooting the painted man who stood there. A second arrow struck ghost father in the arm. Ghost father cried out, but Tomme steadied him, pushed the arrow all the way through to stop its hideous barbs from ripping the flesh anymore. He nocked the same arrow and shot it back. It struck the hunter in the chest. The man snatched at it in panic, and broke the shaft. He sank to his knees and began to scream.

"We have to jump!" Tomme said.

His ghost father said—in the unfamiliar words—*"Tommy, we've got to jump for it!'*

"No, ghost father. There is no time to talk. We must jump! Like this!" He grabbed the man's arm and dragged him to the waterfall. His ghost father urged him on.

They flung themselves into space, and struck the deep pool painfully. They were below the bubbling water for long seconds, but surfaced together and felt the powerful flow of the river carry them into the obscuring leaf of the trees. Tomme laughed mockingly as a large, muscular hunter appeared on the high rocks behind them, and held ghost father's *gun* high above his head. Ghost father saw this and breathed the name "Jacareh."

Then the Fierce People were lost from sight, and Tomme desperately searched for a place to leave the river, before the anacondas and the piranhas scented the blood and sweat of the hunted men.

PART FOUR

The Courage that cries in silence

1

After a while Bill Markham was able to reach out and hold on to the trailing branch of a toppled bamboo. Tommy swam powerfully towards him and grasped the same dead wood, then let his father lean on him. Markham's arm, where he had been shot, was swollen and intensely painful. He felt unreal, giddy. Only panic—and the need for survival—was keeping him conscious.

Both men were in a wretched state, waterlogged and becoming very cold. The feathers in Tommy's hair were bedraggled, limp things that gave his hair the look of a rag doll's.

They were surely out of running range of Jacareh's hunters, now. They had been swept several miles down-water. Above them, through the thinning canopy, Markham could see dark thunderclouds. The whole forest seemed to shiver with the coming storm.

Tommy was speaking to him. His voice was urgent. Markham understood a little of what his son was saying; he recognized the language, but the dialect was quite difficult. The word "piranha" was more than obvious, however. They pulled themselves along the bamboo branches, and slithered up on to the muddy bank. Markham yelled as a large yellow and green snake slithered away into the dank gloom. Tommy said something, a name perhaps, and seemed reassuring about the snake's identity.

"Listen . . ." Tommy said. "The frogs are singing. A big rain is coming."

Markham grasped the sense the second time round. He turned

towards the jungle and heard the dull roar of animal voices, recognizing them at once as frogs. There were other sounds too, sounds of movement, creatures disturbed by the coming storm, racing and slithering to whatever shelter they felt they needed.

"In a big rain," Tommy said slowly, "the big snakes come out of the water."

"Great."

Tommy didn't understand the word and Markham said, in the Indian tongue, "Will we be safe?"

"A raft!" Tommy said. "The river will take us half a day's journey to my village."

Markham rested, shivering in his soaking clothes. He watched his muscular son as the boy—no, hardly a boy anymore—as the young man stripped the branches of the fallen tree and tied them together with liana and vine. He braced the raft expertly. He even fashioned two simple rudders. He tied hand-holds on to the front, and a crude wave-break. All of this took an hour, and the sky darkened even more, and the river began to rumble as water fed into it from further up-stream.

Before they boarded the raft, however, Tommy gathered two handfuls of damp moss. He tied these over his ghost father's arm wound. "No poison, but my father must draw out the fire. We must get to the village quickly."

All Markham understood was "poison, father and village fast." When Tommy repeated his urgent words, using gestures as well, Markham felt a terrible shock as he realized that Tommy meant his father was in the village.

"Tommy! *I* am your father. Don't you remember?"

Tommy smiled sadly, leaning forward. He touched Markham's face, then his own head. "You are my ghost father. You are *dad-dee*. You live in here, in my head. And in my dreams. Now you are here!" He frowned. "My father will tell me what this means."

"Dad-dee *is* your father," Markham protested. He felt dizzy and sick. As he stared at this handsome, intense young man, he could see everything that he remembered about the Tommy of ten years ago. The eyes were the same, the smile was the same. It was his son in every way, and his son was denying him.

"Do you remember your mother? Jean?"

The sound of the frogs grew suddenly louder. Above them, where they crouched on the river bank, some large animal moved deeper into the forest, probably one of the big snakes. Tommy glanced up, then stared back at Markham, frowning. He made no response.

"Your *mother*!" Markham said loudly. "Do you remember Jean? Mommy?"

Perhaps memory stirred in the lost child's mind. Tommy whispered, "Mum-mee," as he stared at his ghost father. For a second he seemed sad, then he smiled broadly. "My mother is Uluru. My youngest mother is Caya. You will like Caya." He seemed to be making a lewd suggestion to Markham, who took a few seconds to piece together what Tommy had said. His youngest mother?

There was no further time to talk. Tommy helped his father to his feet and they dragged the raft to the water. It floated low in the current, and they lay on it, belly down. It turned alarmingly as the current caught it, but Tommy managed to straighten the craft and they began the perilous passage.

Behind them, the storm broke. The sky was laced with brilliant streaks of lightning. The black clouds rolled towards them like waves, overtaking them, and drenching them from above. The water of the river rose. Soon they had no control over the raft at all. They clung on to the flimsy vessel for dear life, at the mercy of the current. They spun swiftly, rocked and threatened to overturn, yet somehow they remained upright, arms looped through the vine hand-holds, and clutching each other like lovers sunbathing.

Markham was astonished at how quickly the water level rose. Ten feet, then twenty, in a matter of minutes. A great boiling front of water had overtaken them and was sweeping on towards the Amazon river itself. Now, as they sailed, they were passing the middle canopy. The land for hundreds of yards each side was in flood, and the torrential downpour was sending a great sheet of destruction through the low forest.

"Ara jaku! Ara jaku!" Tommy yelled. At the same time his grip on Bill Markham became stronger.

"What?" Markham shouted back.

As best he could, Tommy pointed down-stream. Markham looked up through the dark, driving rain. He orientated himself against the whirling wall of forest, and realized that the river, ahead of them, curved sharply to the left. A standing wave of water was breaking over the forest wall exactly at that turn . . .

The raft was flying towards that point. The two men hung on for dear life. The craft sailed up the standing wave and was pitched into the tree-tops. Tommy grabbed the branches desperately and managed to secure himself. Bill Markham slipped down but his fall was broken a few yards below. The river water bubbled through the jungle making it softer and safer to descend to the lower branch line. They crawled away from the river, uncertain as to how far they were above the ground. As soon as they were in a dry place they lay down along the branch, tied themselves secure with vine, and waited for the storm to pass.

2

It took them nearly two days to reach the village. Markham was very weak and needed to rest constantly. When he walked he sometimes walked quite energetically, but mostly needed to support himself on a stick, or on his son's shoulder. Tommy became very frustrated with the slow progress. He debated leaving his ghost father and fetching help, but Markham begged him not to. He panicked at the idea of being left alone, of losing his son so soon after finding him.

The wound in his arm grew even more swollen and turned purple at the edges. The poison in his body—not a fatal poison—made him vomit every few hours. He could keep no food in his stomach, and the strength in his limbs sometimes gave out completely, and at other times burned like fire. Tommy was clearly concerned for him. He administered herbs and poultices from the jungle. He laughed and talked to try to keep his ghost father contented.

He need not have bothered. The simple fact of *being* with his son again was keeping the spirit to live, and to remain conscious, vibrant and vital in the older man.

After a while he stopped calling Tommy by his Western name and called him by the Indian name, which sounded like *To-am-e*—the final vowel having the sound of the vowel of "egg."

At last the two of them came to a place where there were traces of human activity. The fruit of trees had been plucked and the glades and hollows in the forest were trampled and broken. The fire that Tomme found, dead and carefully hidden, had been made by people from the village of Tokowaya. Now Tomme knew exactly where to go, and within a few hours he had begun to emit a bird-like warbling sound, a call to his people, which was eventually answered.

They were in a small space, the thick trunks of trees forming a natural ring about a hollow where once a Grandfather tree had stood. Lightning had struck and killed that tree, and its carcass had been slowly cut and dragged away for fires. Now, the forest floor was rich with stunted pineapple and the glamorous blooms of magnolia. Where the grass grew tall it shimmered silver with the webs of spiders. All the plant life here came up to Markham's shoulders, and he followed Tomme through the soft brush, listening to the conversation of the birds which were not birds, the cries of his son's own people, welcoming him.

They were there, suddenly—five tall, painted Indians, one of them very old, his teeth missing, his body slightly stooped. He alone, this sage among the hunters, wore his hair long, like a woman's. Round his neck he had bones, in his nose he had broad red feathers, like a bizarre moustache. His body was pocked and torn with tattoos, which traced patterns in circles and diamonds and sunbursts, all the way to his knees. On his feet he wore a pair of furry shoes, which looked so like bedroom slippers that Markham laughed when he noticed them.

"This is Wanadi," Tomme said quietly, adding, "my father—"

Wanadi was watching him strangely. The old man smiled then, and said something that Markham thought was, "I remember the edge of the World. I remember you."

One of the other Indians was of almost the same age, but less grandiosely attired. This was Samanpo, Tomme said. The other three were younger, stronger men. All had their hair cropped in the pudding-bowl fashion, all had feathers inserted through the fleshy membranes of their nostrils (and *good God*, Markham thought, Tommy has the same holes!)—all wore decorated penis sheaths, bone earrings and paint. They all carried long, evil-looking spears.

And they all smiled their welcome.

"The Smiling People," Markham said in English. "I've heard of you."

There was much laughter at his strange words. Wanadi said, "You speak the ghost language that Tomme spoke once. The language of the wilderness."

In Tupi, Markham said (with difficulty), "The Fierce People call it The Language of the White Pig . . . and they eat the White Pig . . ."

Samanpo nodded grimly. "They eat all flesh."

Now Tomme stepped forward and drew the pouch from around his neck. He said proudly, "I killed five of the Fierce Ones!"

"Five!" Wanadi said, astonished.

"And I have brought back the Light of the Forest. Look!"

Markham watched amazed as Tomme poured small, beautiful emeralds from the pouch into his hand. The Light of the Forest? Now he noticed the thin green paint patterns on Wanadi's body, and he noticed how the paint sparkled. Did they somehow manage to crush these precious stones and incorporate the dust into their decorations?

Wanadi seemed overwhelmed with the gift. He embraced Tomme, then showed the emeralds to his hunters, saying something that Markham couldn't catch.

Tomme led this old man towards him. His pale, blue-eyed features next to the wizened old Indian made a stark and beautiful contrast. They were holding hands, like lovers. It was an oddly disturbing sight. Tomme said, "Father, this is Dad-dee. This is my ghost father, the one in my dreams."

Wanadi looked solemn. His dark gaze was steady. He watched Markham with an expression that was in no way hostile . . . but which was filled with concern, and with sadness.

"I know of you, ghost father," he said. "You live in my dreams as well. But when a dream is made flesh, trouble is not far behind."

Markham felt instantly cold. He was not frightened, but he began to shake in a way that was not induced by his wound, or by the fever that coursed through his body. He stared at this ancient warrior, with his strange feathers, and skin markings, and cuts, and his weapons, and his bedroom slippers . . .

And he knew. It was as if he had always known this man, this Wanadi. He had never seen him; that day, ten years ago, he had seen nothing but the forest . . . and yet he *had* seen Wanadi. He had looked directly at him, he had seen his eyes and his mouth, and the smile on his face, and the feathers that had decorated his hair. He had seen him and he had *not* seen him.

They were the Invisible People. They had been there, when he and Jean had been frantically searching for their son. They had been within arm's reach. Their breath had touched the Markhams' skin.

And for ten years, Bill Markham had known of this man, this chieftain, only he had never recognized the nature of that knowledge. Wanadi had haunted him, and Markham had been unaware of the ghost.

"It was you," he said slowly. "It was you who took my son."

Wanadi shook his head. "It was you," he said with equal deliberation. "It was you who brought me mine."

Perhaps because the pressure was off, now, since they were safe among the Invisible People, Markham's fever increased and he suddenly felt very ill, and very dizzy. He was hardly aware of being carried out of the forest and across an area of cleared ground, before passing into a circular enclosure, where fires burned brightly. He knew that a cool fabric was applied to his skin. He remembered that a pungent liquid was dribbled between his lips until he swallowed some.

And he remembered a startlingly pretty face looking down at him, as soft hands tugged at his clothes, easing them from his body. The air was cool on his naked skin, but all he could think of, afterwards, was the touch of the girl's fingers as she bathed him, then pushed him back into the hammock, urging him to rest.

Sleep came and was welcomed. His dreams were of water, and running, and fire, and a confusion of symbols of anxiety that made him wake up shouting. She was there, this copper-skinned beauty, stroking his face, his chest, his belly . . . her voice was luxurious and sensuous, and she giggled sometimes, and he laughed too, in the midst of his fever, and reached out to feel the soft, plump flesh that came so close to his own heat-racked body.

In a moment of lucidity he asked her name.

"I am Caya."

"You're an angel. Caya, you're an angel of mercy."

He had spoken in English, and of course his words were meaningless to her. She said, "I am Wanadi's youngest wife."

"Lucky bloody Wanadi," Markham murmured, then said in Tupi, "I hope Wanadi treats you well."

Caya frowned. Markham had had to say, "This ghost father man makes dream that Wanadi cares for you." Perhaps he had said, "Cares at the breast for you"—the wish for happy parenthood—because Caya looked quite astonished, and then giggled unrestrainedly.

She said, "Wanadi and Caya go to the hammock in the way of lightning."

He watched her through the sweat and heat of his fever. What in God's name was she saying? That their hammock kept catching fire?

Ah!

He understood suddenly. He grinned. In English he said, "So you light old Wanadi's fire, do you? Well, again I say, lucky bloody Wanadi."

Caya placed a finger across his lips. "Don't speak the wilderness language," she said.

"Sorry."

"Wanadi has sent me to look after you. If you have need of me, when your fever goes away, I will be by the hearth."

"Need?" he asked in her own language.

She took his hand and placed it gently on her breast. He was too weak to object. "Oh," he said. "That sort of need." He closed his eyes and said in English, "Tell Wanadi that he should be ashamed of himself."

"When you are better, you must call for me," Caya said.

When Markham had worked out the meaning of her words he smiled and nodded, then murmured, "So this is what they mean by a 'fever dream.' "

Caya stayed by the hammock for the rest of the day, wiping the sweat from Markham's face, soothing him gently as he became distressed and disturbed. Uluru brought a bowl of thick medicine, which she trickled between the stranger's lips and managed to get him to drink. The two women exchanged a worried look.

"The wound is clean," Caya said. "The poison is gone. But he doesn't get well."

"We must ask Wanadi to help. He can dance with ghost father's spirit and guide it back to the body."

Caya nodded. It was a good idea.

Wanadi was sitting at Tomme's hearth, smoking a thin pipe from which curls of grey-white smoke rose. Tomme was chewing tobacco and not enjoying it. The two men were talking about Kachiri and how, tomorrow, Tomme should go to her village and make his proposal of marriage.

Uluru walked up to them and crouched by Tomme's fire. "There is a great fire like this one, but it is inside ghost father. It keeps burning. You must come."

Tomme looked concerned. Wanadi stared at his pipe for a moment, then nodded. He placed the pipe by the fire and quickly, surreptitiously, palmed a small, glowing ember. As Uluru walked back to Bill Markham, Wanadi wrapped the ember in a palm leaf. Tomme saw him doing this and questioned him with a frown, but Wanadi just smiled at his son.

Markham was conscious. His eyes were watery and his lips dry; he was in pain—that much was clear—but he watched the chief as the old man approached and tried to smile.

Wanadi stared hard at ghost father, felt his stomach and his cheeks, then shook his head. "He will die," he whispered to Tomme.

Tomme, for a moment, looked like a child again; he stared at Markham and sounded very anguished as he said, "But, father, you are a great healer. You must do something."

Wanadi said, "Sometimes when the forest is on fire, even a great storm cannot stamp out the flames."

"Please try," Tomme said. He came round the hammock and cradled ghost father's head in his hands. Markham stared at him through his liquid gaze, only half seeing. The heat from his skin was enormous. He was shaking violently.

Wanadi said, "Very well. If it can be done, I will do it."

He leaned over Markham and spoke his name until the man turned to stare at him, and registered his presence. "Dad-dee, can you hear me? Ghost father, can you hear the voice of Wanadi?"

Slowly, agonizingly, Markham nodded. He tried to say something but his voice came out as a rasping hiss.

"I will cure you. Do you understand? Ghost father, I will suck the poison and the evil heat out of you."

Tomme added, "He will make you well again. You must believe in him. Wanadi is a great healer."

Feebly, his head turning slightly, Markham whispered, "Tommy . . . stay, Tommy . . ."

"I'm here, ghost father," Tommy said, and took Markham's hand.

"I will make you well," Wanadi insisted. "I will suck the fire out of your flesh. Do you understand?"

Markham nodded. "Yes."

All of Wanadi's wives were gathered round, now, and other women and men of the village. They all wanted to see Wanadi's healing art.

Wanadi stepped closer, stooped over Markham and placed his lips against the dying man's forehead. Then he sucked, he sucked hard and violent. His body racked and twitched with the effort of drawing the deadly fire from the man's body.

Suddenly he pulled away. He slapped his hands to his mouth, then spat violently. The steaming wood ember, glowing slightly red where Wanadi had quickly blown upon it, lay in his hands. He juggled it quickly until it cooled again.

The people watching all shouted their delight. Uluru was most relieved of all, although Caya watched Markham with a happy, knowing look. "There," Wanadi said. "It is the heat that was burning inside you." He picked up Markham's limp hand and dropped the ember into it, then brushed it away as the wood burned him slightly.

"The evil fire—I have sucked it out. It is gone. You will be well again."

"You see!" Tomme said, leaning close to ghost father. "He *is* a great healer."

Markham watched Wanadi through his misty eyes. Then he reached up and feebly touched the old man's arm, drawing him close again. "Why did you take my boy? Why did you take Tommy?"

Wanadi glanced at Tomme, then looked back at Markham. He said, speaking slowly so that Markham would understand, "A long time ago my son was taken from me and killed. I went into the dreamlight and saw the edge of the World. My son's spirit was there, a ghost in a strange body. With my hunters I went to the edge of the World. We watched the Termite People biting down the Grandfather trees and chewing them up. Then my son's spirit walked into the World. It was in the body of a Termite Boy, but he smiled at me and I knew him. I should not have taken him from the dead world, but I had not the heart to leave him."

Markham struggled to understand. But before he could speak, Wanadi had drawn a hand across his eyes, closing them. "Sleep now," he said to ghost father. "When you wake you will be well."

3

Tomme couldn't sleep. Nor could his father. The two of them sat by Tomme's fire throughout the night, smoking, chewing, talking about marriage, the rules and laws of the Invisible People as they related to children and hunting, and most of all talking about love.

Before dawn, Tomme took his marriage hammock and went into the forest. He was aware that his old friend Mapi was following him, but he didn't let Mapi know, he just rapidly ran along the trails, then made an evasive movement and watched the boy trot past. When Mapi had been well and truly thrown from the track, Tomme selected a quiet, secluded glade in the forest and slung the hammock from two trees. He picked flowers and filled the hammock with them. Satisfied that he had sufficiently prepared the marriage bed, he returned to his hearth.

Uluru was awake by now. A fine mist hung in the central space of the village but was rapidly dispersing as other hearths flared into life. The pigs and hens of the compound stirred but were quiet. Wanadi's village was peaceful compared to Tokowaya's, where dogs roamed free and were always noisy in the early hours. Wanadi disliked dogs and had forbidden them.

He and Uluru prepared Tomme for his journey of courtship and marriage. He was given leather shoes which tied round his calves with strips of jaguar fur. These would make running through the forest that much easier. On his head Uluru placed a circlet of white feathers. Wanadi painted the marks of war upon his face, to show that Tomme was now a hunter, but he painted them in bright colors, to show that they were ceremonial. Around his wrists, his mother tied two leather bracelets, from each of which dangled fragments of bone, the bones of the family's ancestors.

One of these would be given to Kachiri, if she accepted Tomme for her husband.

Finally Wanadi presented his son with the elaborate and ornate ceremonial club. Tomme cradled it in his hands, almost nervous to hold it. It was polished and smooth, a carved black lump of hard-wood. Its head-end was rounded and swollen. It tapered to a fine point. The designs carved along its length meant little to Tomme—indeed meant little to anyone in the village; they derived from a long-ago time and the marriage club had been in the village for many generations.

"You know what to do," Wanadi said. "You must do it without hesitation."

Tomme nodded. Then he smiled at his parents, turned and ran from the enclosure.

He followed the line of the river, but kept just inside the forest edge in case some of Tokowaya's people should be fishing or hunting. He ran without stopping, beating the air with the club, getting the feel of it, learning how to strike hard and soft. If he had to kill with the club he must be aware of the best way to use it. He prayed to all the deities of the forest that he would not be challenged.

Very soon he saw Tokowaya's enclosure. Several women were gathering fruit, or digging for vegetables in the clear spaces around the village. Tomme ran through them without pausing, and they all screamed and began to give chase. Two of them he recognized as Kachiri's cousins.

Dogs, pigs and fowl scattered before the sleek young man as he raced into the enclosure. Two hunters shot their arrows at him, warningly, the weapons dropping well short. He brandished the club and they backed away. Around the shabano the young women squealed with fear, delight and anticipation. But all bar one knew that Wanadi's son had not come for them.

For a moment Tomme was confused. The fires burned high and smoke and dust made the whole village seem to shine and shimmer. There was movement around him as if through a gleaming veil.

Which hearth was Tokowaya's?

Suddenly he heard Kachiri cry out. She shouted, "Hide us, father!"

She was letting Tomme know where she was.

He ran to the hearth. Hunters shouted at him, threatened him with spear and bow, but he waved the club at them and they backed away. Two of them shot their arrows into the ground at his feet, but none challenged him.

Tokowaya was an old, wizened man. He was naked but for a head-dress of red and green feathers. He rose slowly to his feet and waved his hunting spear at the stranger. Behind him Kachiri cowered and yelled, covering her breasts with her arms. "Help! Father, he will take me and kill me!"

Tokowaya pressed the point of his spear against Tomme's chest. He growled the words of war of the Invisible People. Tomme made no move; he neither flinched nor threatened.

"I have come to take your daughter. But I give you the Light of the Forest."

He emptied the pouch of emeralds into his hand and held them out to Tokowaya. The old man's eyes lit up, then filled with tears as he stared at Tomme. Slowly his hand came up and the precious stones were exchanged.

"Kachiri no longer has a place at my hearth," he said, his voice breaking with emotion. "But in my heart she will always be there. My spirit will watch over her at all times. If she is ever sent from the hearth of her husband my vengeance will be terrible."

"I hear what you say," Tomme said, "and pledge my fire to Kachiri always."

Now Kachiri screamed and ran from the cover of her father's hearth space. She was an exquisite nude shape, fleeing to the center of the enclosure, with Tomme in hot pursuit. There, she turned and faced him, dark eyes gleaming fiercely, mouth pouting.

"Kachiri, you will tend my fire!" Tomme said.

"Never! My fire is here, with my father."

Tomme raised the club. The warriors around him howled with anger. Arrows thudded softly into the earth beside him. Kachiri's cousins screamed, some tearful, some terrified. Tomme brought the club down softly upon the young woman's head.

"Do it right!" she hissed angrily. The chanting of Tokowaya's hunters grew more urgent.

Tomme raised the club again. This time he struck a firm blow to the top of Kachiri's head. She staggered, smiled, then collapsed to the ground. Tomme didn't hesitate. He scooped her up into his arms and ran with her towards the gate from the village. Kachiri's cousins pursued him, shouting. The hunters continued to shoot at him, the arrows falling short. As he left the village, behind him the women of the enclosure raised their voices in a single, terrible wailing cry.

A drum had begun to beat, a slow, sad sound.

He ran with her as far as he could, following the obvious trails, constantly alert for pursuit. Eventually the strength in his arms had all gone. He stopped and lowered the unconscious woman to the ground, brushing the hair from her face and gently touching her lips.

The marriage hammock was still a long way away. The thought of that journey made Tomme impatient and anguished. Carrying Kachiri, touching her so intimately, had made him need her greatly. The feel of her body, so warm and soft, the arousing, intimate smells that rose from her, all of these things made him want to abandon the tradition.

He shook her by the shoulder. "Kachiri . . . wake up . . . *Kachiri!*"

She didn't move. He watched her eyes and thought he saw the lids flicker slightly. He reached down and stroked her face. He leaned down and rubbed his nose against hers. Still she remained motionless.

"Kachiri! Please wake up. I will give you everything you want: monkeys, stones, furs, skins, honey, feathers . . . children till the day I die . . ."

As he spoke, his voice imploring her to recover, he let his hands drift over her smooth, copper skin, touching her breasts and stomach and thighs, marveling at the sensations they caused in his fingers and in his stomach, and in his deeper places. He was dizzy with desire for the woman who was now his wife.

As he touched her stomach, as he tickled close to the thin bush of damp, dark hair, she shifted and exhaled sharply.

Tomme traced a gentle finger across her skin. "Piranha," he whispered. "Watch out. Piranha . . ."

Kachiri smiled as she lay there, then opened her eyes. She watched Tomme with an adoration that was returned.

"I knew you were awake," he said. "I knew you could hear me."

"I may never be quiet that long again," she said with a giggle;

then bit her lower lip nervously. She reached up for Tomme and he put his arms round her, enfolding her in a fierce, strong embrace.

4

Perhaps because of the breaking of first light, Bill Markham had woken from his feverish sleep in time to see Tomme being dressed in white feathers and boots and presented with a hideous-looking club. Too weak to call out or move, Markham had watched his son run swiftly from the village, his Indian foster-parents watching him sadly. He had no idea what was going on, and after a few minutes his eyes closed again, and he slept.

The illness was with him for the rest of the day, and into the night. He was aware of waking up and feeling cool water on his face. He remembered the smiling features of the woman called Caya, and occasionally the wizened face of the old man. He either heard, or dreamed, a strange ululating chant, during which his body was whipped with colored feathers and a bone rattled noisily. All of these things made him experience nightmares, when he truly slept, in which images from every western film he had ever seen combined confusingly, and chaotically, with his friends, and his family, and even Uwe Werner.

After a while the chanting ended. Night came again, and the village fell quiet.

During the night Markham's fever broke, and his body took control.

He awoke at dawn with a terrible start. The first thing he saw was the sky, still dark and speckled with stars, but beginning to show tinges of blue. The second thing he was aware of was the arm that rested across him. It belonged to Caya. She was curled in the hammock with him, her dark, liquid eyes watching him, her breathing soft.

"Good morning," Markham said awkwardly.

"Yaku, Bill," Caya said.

She was extremely warm and disturbingly well built. Markham shuffled in the hammock, trying to disengage himself from Wanadi's youngest wife, feeling desperately embarrassed. The fire at Wanadi's hearth was already alight, and the village was active. Two pigs were squealing loudly and Markham saw the men grabbing them, and quickly slaughtering them, gathering blood in shallow clay dishes.

It made him shudder to see it, remembering the way Werner had met his end.

His arm still hurt, but was no longer so swollen. His body felt cool, and he was alert and without the racking sensations of nausea that had plagued him since the arrow strike. Although Caya tentatively pinched his flesh, as if trying to say, "Come back," he managed to get his legs out of the hammock and swung to the ground.

With a little mutter of irritation, Caya followed. She stretched and yawned, looking up at the big man.

Markham realized that he was almost naked. A crude, half-concealing loincloth was tied round his waist. Where the rough leather rubbed against his skin he itched. There was a strange green representation of a face on the cloth at the front, and he decided not to ask what it meant.

"I made that for you," Caya said proudly. "Are you hungry? Shall we go to the river and wash?"

Markham looked about the village. The children were already playing, still in the confines of their parents' hearth space. The two pigs were now being dismembered, and the black fowls of the compound were definitely restless. There was much laughter, and a sense of excitement. Caya saw him looking. She said, "We are getting ready for the feast. Tonight. The people of Tokowaya's village will come to eat with us, and dance. It will be a wonderful feast."

"Where's Tommy? I saw him . . . dressed in white feathers—"

Caya admonished Markham in a gentle way, touching her finger to his lips. "He is *Tomme*," she said. "And now he is married. Kachiri is very beautiful. She and I hunted together as children. Now we will work at hearths next to each other." Caya beamed. "I am very happy."

"Married!" Markham said, as he grasped the full sense of Caya's words. The woman took his hand and led him round the village, below the thatch. The smells of manioc soup and baking cassava bread made his mouth water and his stomach rumble. He was starving.

Tomme and Kachiri were curled up together in a hammock, blissfully asleep. Their bodies were untidily streaked with paint, and their hair was full of leaf and twig, as if they had been rolling in a woodpile.

"Tomme needs Kachiri and Kachiri needs Tomme," Caya whispered. "Come. You must eat something."

Markham let himself be led away. Caya gathered up a few biscuits and fragments of smoked meat in a small basket, then held out her hand to ghost father. Markham smiled thinly. He was suddenly aware that Wanadi was sitting in the deep shadow of the hearth space, watching him.

As Caya dragged the reluctant American away from the hearth, towards the village gate, the old man chuckled.

They bathed together in the cool stream, where—Caya told him—Tomme had first seen his new wife. Caya insisted on washing Markham, even though he tried to dissuade her. He eventually sighed with resignation and let the provocative young woman soap him with the scented liquid that she called *oraka*, "dew of the orchid." She shaved him with a piece of sharpened bone. When she offered him some of the smoked meat he was hesitant, but one bite transformed his attitude. It was delicious. There was fish, dried pork, and the sharp-tasting dark meat that he guessed was monkey. He had eaten monkey before, but never with such enthusiasm.

Clean, and with his appetite sated, he lay back on the river bank and watched Wanadi's people as they went about their work and play. Caya plucked flowers from the trees that overhung the stream. In fact, most people seemed to be gathering flowers, and Markham guessed that this was for the wedding feast that evening.

It was strange to think of his son married—and married to one of these exquisite, innocent women. Even though he knew that their forest world was riddled with dangers—from piranha to snakes, from murderous Indian tribes to malaria and measles—it was hard to shake off the idea that he was a guest in paradise. The sun was hot, but the trees afforded some shade; the water was clear, the flowers bright, and the Invisible People seemed utterly and completely content as they talked, laughed and prepared for the celebration.

My son's wedding feast.

He sat up, watching Caya as she jumped for flowers just out of reach. She seemed to be inviting him to watch her. Like all the women of the group, she had a pubescent look about her, a roundness to her body that was unfamiliar to him, so much had he been exposed to the angular elegance of Western fashion. The men were very muscular, their thighs especially. They seemed to emphasize the solidity of their bodies with streaks of paint, but all wore bands of leather, with chips of bone, just above their knees and round their necks.

It was thrilling to him to realize that this particular tribe had never, in thousands of years of existence, been outside the rainforest. Their language was a dialect of the tongue which most Indians in this area spoke, and that meant communication between the Invisible People and other tribes which *had* made contact with the new settlers of the great continent. It had perhaps been the stories that Wanadi and his hunters had heard that had sent them hunting to the very edge of the forest to witness for themselves the destructive nature of the "Termite People."

A sudden frightening thought came to Markham. It was that Wanadi's time in the forest was limited; his people were doomed. Without the forest they would be visible and wretched, and it was only a matter of time before the jungle was chopped from around them. If Tommy was to stay here with them, then he too was doomed, he too would succumb to the jaws of the termites . . .

Behind him, someone called. He recognized Tommy's voice and turned, where he sat, then struggled to his feet.

Hand in hand, Wanadi's son Tomme and his new bride Kachiri walked to the edge of the stream. They were smiling. Tomme carried a blow-pipe and arrows. Kachiri was swathed in flowers and carried a bow.

"Ghost father. You are well again. What did I tell you about my father? He is a great healer!"

"Hello, Tomme. Yes, I am much better."

Tomme embraced Markham warmly. Then Kachiri reached out to touch the white man, smiling. She hesitated for a second, then stretched up on tiptoe and brushed her nose against Markham's.

"I am Kachiri."

"I am Bill."

Tomme said, "We have crushed the stones from the river and once again the Light of the Forest shines in our war-paint." As he spoke he opened the gourd which he was carrying, dipped in his fingers and showed his ghost father the shimmering green paint. He laughed and smeared the paint on his chest in an elaborate spiral. The tiny shards of emerald flashed and glittered brilliantly. Kachiri, too, helped paint Tomme's body, and soon he was decorated from face to feet. He grinned at Markham again. "Now not even the monkeys will see me. Not even the trees. Nothing will see me when I hunt. I will be truly invisible."

As Kachiri went to the water and washed her hands, Markham finally managed to say to his son what had been on his mind for hours, at least, if not years.

"Tommy—*Tomme*. I have come to take you home. I have been searching the forest for you for years. Many times I have been in the forest calling for you."

Tomme watched him, frowning slightly. "Ghost father, this *is* my home."

"You had another home once, Tomme. I have come to make you remember that home. I want you to remember everything. Your mother, your sister Heather. California. Your friends in California. We all want to see you again. We've all been waiting so long."

Tomme shrugged. He was not being dismissive, he was just uncertain as to what his ghost father was saying. The words confused him. He vaguely remembered ghost mother, but these other things were just meaningless names to him, now . . . and the hunt was waiting! The monkeys were waiting impatiently for the chase, and the Light of the Forest glowed upon his body. He could feel the spirits from the forest floor seeping into his body through the soles of his feet, making him anxious to dance the ritual hunt-dance, the dance of death.

Kachiri had heard Markham's careful, quiet words. She crouched down by Tomme and rested her hand on his shoulder. "Ghost father, he belongs to me now. I am his woman. We share fire together, we share ancestors, now." She raised her wrist and the bone shards gleamed. Markham didn't understand the full significance but guessed she was showing him the Invisible People's equivalent of a wedding ring.

He began to feel very angry, and very frustrated. Had he spent ten years of his life trying to rescue Tommy only to have his son regard him as a dream? Grimly he realized that he had overlooked—deliberately, of course—any consideration of what would have been happening to Tomme in the forest, during those long years.

In his mind, he knew, he had always had an image of Tomme—or *Tommy*—still wearing the ragged remains of his western clothes, huddled in the corner of a hut, crying and miserable. Women brought him food, the children peered at him, mocking him, he was always kept warm, and he never understood the fluting language of his captors.

For ten years.

Markham allowed himself a bitter smile. Such self-deception, such callous ignorance. But how could he have truly known the changes that were happening to his son?

His son. Dammit! These people *stole* his son. Tommy should at least have the chance to choose, now, where he would prefer to be. And he couldn't choose when so much memory of his real, and first world, had been obliterated from him.

"I must help you remember," Markham said. "I must help you remember the home you had with me, with Mommy, with Heather. Your home in the city—"

"In the wilderness," Tomme said, smiling. "My home in the Dead World. But I don't wish to remember it. I have my own fire here, and my Kachiri, and my children will live here."

Abruptly he rose to his feet and waved the bunched arrows and pipe darts that he held. "I must hunt. I must bring back monkey and river fish for my wedding feast. I am a happy man, ghost father, because I have Kachiri, and now I have *three* fathers. That makes me very proud."

"Three fathers?" Markham asked, confused.

"You, my ghost father. And Kachiri's father, Tokowaya. And my real father . . ." As he said this he turned and smiled at Wanadi, who had approached the group by the river without sound. Markham stood and stared at the old warrior, who was painted as brilliantly green as his son.

Wanadi said, "No father could be happier than me. You are not just a man, Tomme, you are a killer of men, and all must see it."

He stepped up to Tomme and painted four thin red lines across his torso, using one finger and dye from a small pot. Then he gave the pot to Kachiri, and held Tomme by the shoulders, beaming at him.

Markham's anger exploded and he roughly pushed the old Indian aside.

"You have *one* father, Tommy. And that is me. *I* am your father. This man stole you! He took you from me, from 'Mommy.' "

Tomme just watched Markham implacably. Wanadi, too, seemed unperturbed by the outburst. He said, "Yes . . . yes . . . I always knew we could tame a termite child. But that he should become such a warrior—that's more than a father could hope for."

The two of them turned and began to walk along the water's edge towards the jungle. Markham followed quickly after them and grabbed Wanadi roughly by the shoulder. The old Indian stopped and watched the white man.

Markham said, "I speak to you as father to father. I want my son to see where I live . . . and how I live—and then he can choose."

Tomme was impatient to go hunting. "I live here," he said. "This is my home. Come on, father. The monkeys won't wait all day."

Seething with frustration, Markham said to the other man, "Are you the chief?"

Wanadi nodded. "That's what they say."

"Then *you* tell him. Tell him to come back with me, just for a while. To visit . . ."

But Wanadi just smiled and turned to follow Tomme again. He said quietly, but audibly, "If I tell a man to do what he does not want to do, I am no longer chief."

The two Indians walked swiftly away from him. Markham watched them go. To his astonishment they suddenly blurred with the forest wall and disappeared, although the sun, reflecting brightly off some polished surface, suggested that they had not yet entered the jungle.

Behind Markham, Kachiri and Caya were giggling together, discussing ghost father in deliberately lewd terms. Kachiri ran quickly back to the village, leaving Markham alone with Caya, who began to rub flowers on to her body, making a cooing, inviting sound which made the man feel very apprehensive, very alone. He was on the point of tears, confused and angry, a visitor in this idyllic place, but a visitor who had no part to play.

5

By the time Tomme returned from the hunt later in the day, the village was in a state of great excitement as preparations for the night's celebration were made, and Bill Markham was exhausted, mostly from keeping the persistent and voluptuous Caya at arm's length.

He crouched by Tomme's hearth, helping with the mixing of bright dyes ready for the ceremonials. Uluru was making bread. The uncovered part of the enclosure was being decked out with flowers. Eight large poles, all carved with faces and figures, had been erected in this space, and small smoking braziers placed by each of them. If these were in any way totemic, thc cxact animal nature escaped Markham, since most of the carvings were unreal and nightmarish.

All around the enclosure different foods were being prepared; at one hearth an exquisite dish of fragrant fruit; at another, strips of smoked meat; at a third, a great vat of amber liquid; at Samanpo's hearth, close to Wanadi's, manioc soup was being made, and much spitting was in progress.

The two sacrificed pigs were already being slowly roasted, but when Tomme returned, Wanadi close behind and clearly a little breathless and tired, their catch—four different types of monkey, a spear full of fish and four fat, golden snakes—was taken with much excitement, and distributed among the hearths.

It was clear enough which food was the most valued among the Invisible People.

Watching his son, as the lean and strong young man joked and mock-fought with others of the young hunters, Markham knew that the decision—sad and painful though it was—the decision which he had made was the correct one. Tears filled his eyes again, as they had a few hours earlier when the full hopelessness—or rather, pointlessness—of his mission had come home to him. Caya saw the sadness and stopped her incessant chatter and play. She had only been trying to help him relax, to feel a part of the community, and perhaps at last she too recognized the necessity to give up.

Tomme danced quickly round two of the grotesque totems and elicited much laughter with his antics. He tossed his arrows to a young man, whom Markham had heard referred to as "Mapi," and passed his blow-pipe to Kachiri. Behind him, Wanadi said something, perhaps complaining about the fuss being made of Tomme and the lack of attention that he himself was receiving. He was suddenly surrounded by people, all of them elaborately and deliberately commenting on his great hunting prowess.

With a shout and a pretence of anger, he scattered them.

Tomme belongs here.

The thought made Markham choke with grief. It would be very hard leaving this place, but he knew—he had decided—that leave he must. He would wait for his son's wedding feast, and then go. The longer he stayed the harder it would be to return to the city.

Followed by Mapi, Tomme came over to where Markham was sitting. He was smiling with contentment as he approached, but he frowned when he saw ghost father's sad expression. He said something to Mapi and the younger man laid Tomme's weapons on the ground and walked away from the hearth. Tomme came over and sat beside Markham.

For a while they remained in silence. Then Tomme said, "Sometimes, when it rains, for many days we cannot hunt and we go hungry. We lie in the hammocks and the children cry. In those times we tell our dreams. I dream often about you, ghost father. And about my ghost mother."

"Do you, Tomme?" Markham stared hard at his son. There was a glimmer of hope in his heart, a moment's excitement. But it passed as rapidly as it had come. Tomme had sensed his sadness, and was now trying to show some concern, that was all.

Tomme said, "There is a river without water. We are in a canoe but it has a roof."

Bill Markham laughed gently. "That's a car, Tomme. We call it a car. You always wanted to sit behind the wheel of our car, to pretend to drive it."

To communicate these advanced ideas was not easy. He had said, "Sit behind the circular paddle and sail the 'car.' "

Tomme remembered more of his rain dreams, now. He said

excitedly, "And I can see through the walls of this canoe . . . the walls are made of hard water . . ."

Walls made of hard water? Ah! Windows. There was no way to explain this to the son who had forgotten, so Markham just nodded.

Shaking his head, Tomme said, "It is a very funny dream. We all laugh and forget our hunger. I tell the people many dreams, many stories." He looked at ghost father proudly. "When I am old, like my father, like Wanadi, I shall be a great storyteller."

Markham watched the young man and felt his eyes sting. He smiled. "I'm sure you will be the best storyteller in the world, Tomme."

Tomme nodded acknowledgment. "Thank you, ghost father. I shall never forget those words." He leaned closer, thinking about something, then straightened up, a decision made. "Would you like me to tell you a story now? It's one I remembered on the hunt today. I shall tell it to Kachiri as my special gift to her."

"I would be honored," Markham said.

He had expected nothing. He had expected a hunting tale. He had not expected either to understand it, or to like it. What Tomme said next, then, came as a terrible shock to him. He was unable to speak, or murmur sound, for long minutes.

"This," Tomme said dramatically, "is the story of the Terrifying Anteater! It is an ancient dream story, first told in the dreamlight time, when the people were still hidden in the trees of the forest . . ."

The Awful Anteater . . . his own story to Tommy and Heather, the family joke . . . Tommy didn't even remember that it was he, his ghost father, who had first invented this tale, and its title!

"At this time, the World was so big that no one hunter could have run from end to end of it in a single lifetime. On all sides the World was surrounded by fire, although the great waters waited outside the fire, ready to form the rivers. When the Anaconda came into the World, gouging out the river-ways and allowing the water to flow freely, so there came the Great Ones, every animal of the World, all of them huge . . ."

The Invisible People at this time were just beginning to learn the ways of the hunt-trail. Many of them were still waiting in the thick trunks of the trees, or the grey faces of the rocks, but a few had begun to run, and by running, and breaking down the plants of the forest, they marked out the sacred spirals, and the patterns of the hunt, and of belonging. This was the way the first village was formed.

Half a day's walk from this first village an old man, who had left his rock far sooner than he should, had made a garden. He had made the garden by cutting down four Grandfather trees. This took him half of his life. Then he had cut the rest of the forest from the ground. This had taken him half of the life that remained to him. In the clearing he planted flowers and vegetables, and he tended them with great care, even though he never gathered them, or allowed the people of the village to gather them.

At this time, ghost father, the Great Ones were looking for their final places of rest. Snakes and monkeys, ants and armadillos, pigs and macaws, all of them passed by the garden of the old man and laughed at his foolishness. But then came the anteater. The old man's garden was on the same spot where the anteater was destined to sit down and die. When the great anteater came into the garden the old man chased it off.

"This is *my* place!" the anteater said.

"This is my *garden*!" the old man shouted back, and he struck the animal with his club.

"This is my special place to die," the anteater said. "You can choose from all the World to make your garden, but only this place has been put aside for me."

"This is my garden," yelled the old man, still waving his heavy club. "I have spent three-quarters of my life making this garden. I have cut down trees, I have cleared the bushes, I have planted seeds. This place is mine, now. You have the whole forest in which to find a place to die."

The anteater was frantic. It was bleeding from the club wound, but still it persisted. "If you had asked the Great Ones you would have known that this was my special place. You are the Rock and Tree people. You have only just come into the World. If you had asked any other of the Great Ones they would have told you that this place is sacred."

The old man said, "The earth here is good. The seeds develop well. Why should I worry about anything except my garden? As long as the garden does well, that is all that matters."

"You are wrong," the anteater said. "Your garden will do well wherever you grow it. It will do best when you grow it in the proper place. This is *my* place, not yours, and yet you pretend to own it. Your garden will flourish, but I will not die properly. If you had planted your garden a day's walk to the south, your garden would have flourished and I would have found peace."

"Why is this place so special to you?" the old man asked. "Why don't *you* go a day's walk to the south and die?"

"I was first in the World," the anteater said. "My resting place was told to me many years ago. I cannot change as easily as you. In this way I am weak and you are strong. But when you deny my rights to my own resting place it is you who are weak, and you who will die."

The old man thought about this. "I have spent three-quarters of my life clearing this garden to plant it. I shall stay."

The anteater said, "I have spent *all* of my life seeking this garden. If you plant it, you will destroy more than just this anteater."

The old man was impatient. He struck the anteater repeatedly on the head and killed it. But he was too frightened to touch the body of the animal and he left it there. For a while he continued to plant the garden around the body of the anteater, but soon the jaguars came and crunched up the body for the meat. Then the carrion birds descended and stripped the last shreds of flesh from the corpse. They flew up into the trees and watched the old man. The monkeys came from the forest and gathered up the bones of the anteater and carried them away. Then the flies came and sucked the remaining juices from the ground. Each creature that came to eat stayed and watched. The old man waved his club at them, but he could not reach them. Soon he realized why they were staying. This was not his garden at all. They were waiting for him to die so that they might eat him; then the trees would grow back, and the jungle, and the anteater would be regurgitated and allowed to rest.

All the creatures of the forest, and all the creatures from outside the forest, have a proper place to live and a proper place to die.

"That's a good story," Markham said. Tomme smiled broadly, pleased with the compliment. Markham thought, *Aesop's Fables, the* Jungle

Book *and my own anteater story. Tomme is re-creating the myth-world of the Invisible People from his bedtime reading.*

Memories of Tomme, as a tiny child, scampering into bed clutching a book nearly as big as his own body, and waiting for Jean and Bill to come and sit and read with him, sudden memories of that time in California made Markham's eyes water. Those images were all he would have, now, and yet they were all any parent would have; but for the Markhams, whose son was still alive, they would be as poignant and as harrowing a set of recollections as if their son was dead.

"Why are you so sad, ghost father?" Tomme asked, and Markham realized that the boy had been watching him closely.

"I've been looking for you, Tomme. Ten years. Ten hunt-trails. Looking for you all over the World, and now the searching is finished."

Tomme nodded. He seemed to understand. "Yes," he said. "It is good to hunt. Sometimes we track an animal for many days, and when we catch it we are happy with the catch, but sad that a good chase is finished."

Markham smiled. He said, "It was a good story. Kachiri will enjoy it. Everything has its proper place and your place is with her . . ."

"Tonight our place is with you, and with the fire. It will be a good feast."

6

The fires burned high and bright round the sides of the enclosure. The sound of laughter and chatter was loud in the warm night. The air was filled with a rich variety of smells: roasted meats, smoked fish and, most pronounced of all, the perfume of flowers. There were flowers everywhere, brilliantly colored blooms of all sizes. Markham was wreathed with crimson and yellow orchids and his hair was stiff with feathers; it seemed that every young woman in the two villages, married or unmarried, waited to put a feather in his hair and depart, giggling.

Discreetly he removed as many of them as he could. He danced a little, but still felt quite weak. He was content to sit at Wanadi's hearth, between Wanadi and Tokowaya, Kachiri's father. A pipe was passed repeatedly between the three of them, the three fathers, watching their children with smiles of pride and pleasure. Markham dutifully puffed on the pipe, but found the taste sour and the smoke cloying. He was happier drinking the warm, scented ale that had been prepared for the ceremony. Now he was light-headed and dizzy; not sad, just very distant.

In the village, the drums began a slow steady rhythm and everyone but the three fathers stood up and went into the middle of the enclosure. They formed into two snake-like columns of dancers, three abreast, the men in one with Tomme at their head, the women in the other led by Kachiri. The dance was a strange one, with the column of men circling slowly and steadily in time to the drum beat, round the winding spiral of the women. Every one of the dancers moved in perfect unison—a steady, bobbing dance, a slow march round the enclosure and between the totem poles, in which the dancers became more and more complexly intertwined. And suddenly, Tomme and Kachiri were dancing next to each other, and the men and women were pairing off, laughing and joking as they took each other's hands.

Now the newly married couple led the whole array of dancers and they slowly approached the three "old men" by the fire, standing before them as they danced from foot to foot in time to the drums, their faces radiant with paint and pleasure. Tomme looked magnificent in his head-dress of feathers and his robe of flowers and broad leaves, all tied together with vine. Kachiri was swathed in flowers, and this simple garment served to emphasize her natural beauty.

Markham felt disturbed and deeply proud of the young couple; they were like hunters out of Eden—bold, brilliant and beautiful.

When the dance was finished Kachiri joined her cousins, and the dancers from the two villages gathered round the fires for a further session of eating and drinking. Tomme came over to his father's hearth and sat with the three men. He was drunk, both with alcohol and with love. While he smoked tobacco in the crude bamboo pipe he could hardly take his eyes off Kachiri, as she and her cousins played a chase game around the totem poles in the enclosure.

Wanadi said to Markham, "We call that the Chase of the White Flower. Kachiri is a woman, now, and this feast tonight is the last time she may play such games with her friends. They chase her to stop her being a child; she runs because she would always like to be carefree. She is the white flower. When she is caught she will become the red orchid." Wanadi chuckled and winked at Markham. "When she is a red orchid she will play a very different game."

Markham wanted to say, "But she's already been playing it," but he resisted, content to let the rituals and beliefs of the Invisible People unfold themselves to him without being too closely questioned.

Instead he said to Tomme, "I must leave. Tomme, this is not my place, and I must go back to what you call the Dead World."

"The wilderness," Wanadi whispered, and Markham realized that the old man was shocked by the thought that anyone could willingly return to such an awful realm.

Tomme nodded thoughtfully, looking a little crestfallen. Then he said, "Ghost father, you will always be welcome at my fire. And ghost mother too."

"Thank you, Tomme. Perhaps, in time, we *shall* come and visit."

Wanadi was still very perturbed by Markham's decision. "Daddee," he said, using Tomme's affectionate name for his ghost father, "why go back to that terrible place? You will become a ghost, again. You can stay here with us. We will teach you to become invisible. You will become a great hunter, a great warrior. And Tomme will have both of his fathers near to his hearth."

Bill Markham smiled, then reached out and gently squeezed Wanadi's arm. "Thank you," he said. "I cannot tell you how much I would like to do that, to stay here, to become one of my son's people."

"Then do it. The ghosts in the wilderness will not miss you."

"Ghosts can love people too," Markham said without thinking, and then laughed. Where had he heard that before? And he remembered suddenly, the picnic, ten years ago, when they had been eating sandwiches and Heather had been playing with an ant. Ants can love people too, she had said, and Tommy—who disliked most forms of creepy-crawly—had watched her in utter disgust.

He met Tomme's eyes, now, and saw how the young man was frowning. Perhaps, for that instant, Tomme too was remembering the picnic, and that moment of affection shown by his sister for one of the lesser beasts of the world.

Wanadi was chuckling heartily. "I had never thought of that," he said. "Perhaps ghosts go hunting . . ." he and Tokowaya shuddered with mirth at the thought of it. "Perhaps they get married . . ." more chuckling. "They dance ghost dances and warm themselves by ghost fires."

The old men slowly came back to reality, wiping the tears of laughter from their eyes. Then Wanadi became serious again. "Even so, you are more than a ghost, now. You are a man of courage. I see well where Tomme's great heart has come from. It would make us all very proud to have you live with us. And you can visit the ghost world as often as you like. Please, Dad-dee. Do stay!"

Markham shook his head. "I can't, Wanadi. My family is there. It is where I belong. Tomme has a mother there. A ghost mother, yes, but she remembers Tomme, and misses him greatly." It was not easy for him to say what he said next. He glanced at Uluru, the proud older woman, who was sitting close by and nursing one of Pequi's children while the younger woman danced with her friends.

Uluru smiled at him, but there was a great sadness in her eyes, and Markham was uncertain as to where, or to whom, that sadness was directed.

He went on, "I promised Tomme's ghost mother that I would bring him back. We have always known that to find him would be the longest and hardest search. But we never realized that even if we found him we would still have lost him."

Wanadi simply smiled. He returned the gesture of affection, the gentle squeeze of the arm, followed by a little nod of understanding. "Your heart is torn. If you take him you will wish you hadn't, because you know now that Tomme belongs in the World. If you don't take him, however, you will always wish you had . . ."

It was a simple truth too terrible to bear, too frightening to contemplate for the moment. Markham noticed how Tomme and his Indian father exchanged a conspiratorial glance, a quick unspoken word between them.

Then Wanadi said, "Ghost father, you are a man of courage. You have traveled far into the World. You have shown the Fierce People that you have, in you, the spirit of a great hunter, of a great warrior. But you have shown the Invisible People that you have a spirit even greater than that. You have the courage that cries in silence. In here—" he tapped Markham's chest gently, and smiled. "Dad-dee . . . that is not a courage that I have, and I envy you."

"There is nothing to envy," Markham said, but Wanadi held up his hand, saying to Markham to be silent for a moment.

"You are wrong. Your visit here, your courage, will now become a part of the spirit of this village. You will be spoken of for many generations. Your son—Tomme—will tell stories about you, and they shall never be forgotten . . ."

Wanadi reached to the small pile of pipes by the three men and picked up a strangely carved tube, in whose bore a green dust sparkled. He raised it in front of Markham and smiled. "You came a long way into the World, to its very heart. Now you must go further, and see more. You will run through the forest like the animal that inhabits you, and you will know the forest in a way that is very different. This is our gift to you."

Markham hesitated, not liking the implication that he was to smoke the dust in the pipe. "I'm not sure," he said, but Tomme hissed at him, pleading with him.

"Accept our gift, ghost father. You will travel fast. You will be back at the wilderness before one dream is finished. You will become the being that is inside you. Don't be afraid, ghost father. I shall hold you, and I shall stay with you until you are home again."

Tomme came round behind Markham and cradled his head. Markham squirmed a little, uncertain and unsure, but he felt weak and not in command of his actions. Wanadi's voice had a hypnotic effect upon him, and when the old man approached him with the pipe he remained quite still.

Wanadi smiled at him. "Goodbye, Dad-dee."

This is happening too quickly! I need time, a little more time, to say goodbye to Tommy. I'm not ready yet!

Uluru called to him, "May your journey be a safe one, ghost father."

"Tomme . . ." Markham said, and reached up to his son's cradling hands, squeezing them. Tomme leaned closer and whispered, "You will go into the dreamlight. I shall always be with you. I shall always remember you . . . my father—"

"Tommy! I love you!"

Wanadi pushed the thin tube against Markham's nostril.

"Time to go," Tommy whispered gently.

Wanadi blew down the tube. Something astringent and choking poured into Markham's lungs. His chest heaved, his vision blurred. The village became shrouded by a green mist. His body felt as if it was on fire. The faces around him receded, the sound of the fires grew until the roar and crackle of the burning wood was deafening.

He opened his mouth to scream . . .

The jaguar growled . . .

He was running through the emerald forest, moving effortlessly through the web and weave of the jungle. He was aware of a thousand smells; they tickled and teased his senses, but could not disguise the one simple scent at their centre: the fear of his prey, running ahead of him, desperate to escape.

His body was a celebration of animal power. He could feel the way his muscles moved beneath the loose skin, superbly lithe, able to cope with his weight, and his speed, and the bruising strike of branches and roots upon that body, as he leaped and ducked and raced in pursuit of the smaller animal. He extended his claws. They emerged like ivory talons, sensuously stretching the skin and flesh. They gleamed before his eyes as he pulled himself into the branches of a great tree.

He lay there, above the moist, warm floor of the forest. He watched the movement of birds and snakes, he listened to the screeching, howling sounds of the jungle. He listened to the sound of his own breath.

He went after his prey again, bounding through the crowded spaces, creeping over rocks, and sliding cautiously down thick tangles of roots. The smell of death grew stronger in his nostrils.

He made the kill. He feasted on the warm, sweet meat. He chewed on the thin bones, feeling them break between his teeth, savoring the bloody marrow. Satiated, his belly distended, he moved more slowly towards the smell of water.

He drank at the pool. An Indian hunter crouched on the other side of the water and watched him. He knew the danger of these forest hunters, and when he had drunk his fill he quickly returned to the concealing gloom of the jungle.

Again he ran. The dreamlight bathed him softly. The leaves crackled and whispered as he passed beneath them; the great trees watched him in majestic silence.

And suddenly, ahead of him, the World was broken by the roar of a great animal. Its vast jaws chewed on the forest. It swept into the World from the wilderness, its head swaying from side to side as it consumed all the life it saw. He cowered back, ears flat, jaws open, hissing his warning. But the lumbering monster came on, looming over him, screamimg at him, finally . . .

. . . falling silent.

"Senhor! Oi, Senhor! Quem é vôce?"

Markham opened his eyes. He immediately felt sick. His head felt like lead. Three faces peered down at him, and he struggled to sit upright.

"Where am I?"

"Inglês?" One of the faces came closer. "Hey, buddy. What you do, huh? Where you do in this forest here?"

He was naked, totally naked. He was lying on a crude stretcher. An arrow, its flights made of green and red feathers, was stuck in the ground beside him. The men who watched him so anxiously were foresters, mestizo Indians, alarmed by the fact that in the middle of the virgin wood they had suddenly found a naked white man, peacefully sleeping.

The monster in his dream had been the bulldozer. It towered over him now, its scooping jaws raised high. Its flanks were yellow. The AmazCo emblem was clearly distinguishable upon its side.

Beyond the savaged trees Markham heard the roar of trucks; and the tinny whine of chainsaws. AmazCo were building a road, a great red cut through the forest, a wide track for industry.

Markham struggled to his feet. The workmen helped him. One of them offered him a jacket and he wrapped it around his waist.

He looked away from the road to where the forest was still a dark place, its secrets intact . . . for a few minutes more.

From that yellow-streaked gloom a bird called to him—an eloquent, beautiful song.

7

Before he was led away, into his own world, Markham had looked for several long seconds directly at Wanadi and Tomme as they stood just outside the forest. Both men had smiled, but Markham, with his ghost's eyes, was unable to see them.

Tomme called to him, and he seemed to recognize that. He waved briefly.

When he was gone from sight, Wanadi led the way back to the trail. He was sad, and he was also tired. Samanpo and several others were waiting for him. They had helped carry the unconscious, dreaming man to the nearest road, over a day's trot from the village. It was not easy, moving with a man of Markham's build slung in a hammock. It was not easy keeping him asleep, either.

"It's a big track," he explained to the others. He looked up through the canopy. "It follows the flight trail of the curawaya bird. But it can't be for the curawaya. They don't need tracks." He sighed. The reason for such a wide road, cutting so straight through the World, was very hard to see.

They began the long walk back to the village.

Towards the end of the day, when Wanadi had sent two hunters ahead of the group to seek out a good place to make an overnight camp, a number of dark birds gathered in the sky above them. Wanadi watched them, but said nothing. Tomme had seen them too, and he had seen the look of apprehension on his father's face.

"What do they mean?" he asked. "Are they an omen?"

"It's hard to tell."

They had found a clearing. Samanpo lit a small fire and cooked the flesh of a small monkey that he had shot just before dusk. Wanadi didn't eat. He said he wasn't hungry. Above the group, the canopy was restless with the sound of wings, as if a giant bird was struggling there.

As the others rested, Wanadi pulled the teeth from the tiny monkey's skull. He cradled them in his hand, then shook them and scattered them at his feet. He stared at the bones in silence, and he stared for a long time. Then he rubbed them into the ground with his foot and looked distractedly into the darkness.

"Father . . . ?"

"Get some rest, Tomme. We will continue before daybreak."

They ran through the forest, through the heavy, stinking mist. They were sleek, gleaming shapes, ducking and weaving through the tangled growth, chanting in rhythm as they ran, stopping every few hundred paces to listen.

As the light of the day began to filter through the canopy, they became dark silhouettes against the shafting yellow. They would appear from gloom, pass rapidly across a brightly lit clearing, and vanish again.

No one asked Wanadi what he had seen, what he knew, what the omens were. They just followed him aware that something was wrong.

And something was very wrong indeed.

From the top of a ridge they could look down towards the river valley where the villages of the Invisible People lay hidden. Wanadi gasped with shock, and Tomme fell to his knees as he stared across the green forest to the thick column of smoke rising from the enclosure where they had spent their lives.

"A raid on our village!" Samanpo cried.

"It will be the Fierce People," Wanadi said, shaking his head sadly.

Tomme cried out, "Kachiri! Kachiri!" and led the group at a fast run, not stopping for breath, nor to listen, until they came flying out of the forest's edge, close to the river.

The enclosure was a smoking ruin. The gateway was still burning, a small fire on the last of the log pile. Heavy ash and dust filled the air. The stink in the air was of smoke and charred flesh.

A dishevelled, smoke-blackened figure came running from hiding, shouting at the men. It was Mapi. He was clutching an infant in his arms, and Tomme recognized the child as Pequi's. Mapi's face was tear-streaked, and he cried again as he found the men, this time with relief.

"It was the Fierce Ones. They came before dawn."

Tomme rushed through the remains of the gate, screaming Kachiri's name. The other hunters followed. Wanadi walked slowly and sedately, clutching his spears and arrows, his face a grey, hard mask.

Tomme was shouting, "She's not here. Kachiri isn't here. Nor Caya . . ."

Wanadi had eyes for only one thing. He walked over to where Uluru lay, by the remains of her hearth. She looked as if she was sleeping. She was quite peaceful in death, and Wanadi bowed to her, then knelt down beside her. After a while he placed a small leaf over the round wound in her chest. He bent low and whispered something in her ear, then stood up and called Mapi to him.

Tomme came too, and now he saw Uluru and was shocked. He sank to his knees and wept bitterly for a while, but when Wanadi placed a hand on his shoulder he stopped this show of grief, wiped his eyes and stood up. "Where are the others?" he said.

Samanpo, hiding his own grief well, said, "The young children are dead, all but Pequi's child. Two are not here, but they have been taken for the fire. Eight of us are missing—the women, including Kachiri."

Tomme still was too shocked, too distraught to think straight. He looked around the enclosure, appalled again at the scatter of bodies, their flesh laid open with spears. And with something else . . .

Mapi said, "There was a noise like thunder. The leader had a black weapon that spat smoke and killed without arrows."

Tomme remembered Jacareh, standing on the rocks above the river waving ghost father's gun. But the gun had had no fire. Where had Jacareh and the Fierce People obtained the fire?

It didn't seem to matter. They had found the invisible arrows that could be used in the weapon, and they had come and killed everyone in the village. Everyone but the women.

"It is not like the Fierce People to take the women for their own village," Wanadi said. "They have taken them for another purpose."

"What purpose?" Tomme whispered. He dreaded Wanadi saying, "For the fire."

But Wanadi said, "We must follow them and find out. We must capture them, and bring the young women back to us. We must do this soon. But first we must honor the dead."

The fire began to burn brightly. Tomme had made it, using wood from the forest, wood from the enclosure, and the remains of the spirit-trees, the carved poles about which he and Kachiri had danced only a few days before.

When the fire was high, Wanadi took up the bone knife, which he had found in the ashes of his hearth space, and prepared the corpses of the dead for burning. He alone did this, as he was chief of the Invisible People. But when he carried Uluru to the fire he stumbled and fell; when Tomme went to him he found that his father was crying so badly that he could not get up. Tomme, then, carried the remains of his mother to her final resting place.

The heat endowed the dead with life-like movements. Uluru's body began to rise; others flapped their limbs. All of the dead opened their eyes and mouths in a scream that sounded only in the dreamlight.

"They call for revenge," Tomme said bitterly.

Wanadi agreed with him.

"Why do we sit here, then?" Tomme shouted, suddenly angry, suddenly frightened again. "Why do we wait?"

Samanpo, Wanadi and the others ignored him. Only Mapi, crouched outside the circle of the men, half rose in excitement, ready to support the call to war.

Wanadi said, "The fire will set free their souls to the stars. And what is left of the dead must be crushed and crushed again, until it is dust. When this is done, Tomme . . . when this is done, and the dead are with us again, then we will hunt. Then we will revenge the dead."

Tomme relaxed. In his mind he had a confusion of images: of Kachiri, of his ghost father, of the eagle that was his secret being, of childhood pleasures, with his mother Uluru singing to him—all of these sights he watched now, in the yellow bite of flame and fire.

When the dead were burned, the men stroked through the ashes for the shards of bone. When these were gathered they were placed in the village's hollow stone, and Wanadi crushed them until they were fine dust. Then he went to his own hearth and dug down into the red soil. Soon he found a wooden box, a small thing. In the box was more ash, more dust. "In here," he said, "is the dust of all those who went before us, even of the first man and the first woman."

He pinched up a large amount of the newly dead and sprinkled them into the box. He closed the lid and shook the box hard. Then he opened it again and pinched out some dust, and placed it in a small clay beaker.

"Now they rest with their ancestors. We shall bury the box again. If none of us returns from the hunt, no one will ever find it."

When this simple task was done, Samanpo made a thin soup out of the remaining supplies that the band carried. Each man, then, cut a small slash in his arm and dripped the blood into the broth . . .

"You too, Mapi. Your blood too."

"I am not a man. I have not yet undergone mv hunt-death."

Wanadi smiled at him sadly. "You have undergone the worst hunt-death ever. You are a man now, and must behave as one."

Uncertain, yet excited, Mapi crept forward and cut his flesh. When he looked up at Tomme, Tomme was smiling.

"Hello, friend," Tomme said.

"Hello, Tomme," Mapi whispered.

The dust of the dead was sprinkled into the broth and blood. Wanadi raised the cup in both his hands. "We will drink this in memory of what we have been." He sipped from the cup and passed it to Tomme, saying, "And in love of all those who went before us, and who will now live inside us."

Last to drink was Mapi. He was starving. There was much broth left inside the cup. As the rest of the hunters rose to their feet and—weapons in hand—began to run towards the forest, Mapi gulped the warm soup down. When he had finished he grabbed a spear, and a bow, and the bone knife which Wanadi had left.

He raced after the other men.

PART FIVE

Into the Dead Forest

1

Since he had lost track of time he had no idea how far from the village of the Invisible People the new road was being constructed. He had dreamed vividly of being a jaguar, running through the jungle, and he could well imagine that Wanadi and Tomme had been carrying his sleeping body throughout that strange experience.

But a day? Two days? His beard was coarse; he had shaved reasonably closely that day in the river, with Caya. More particularly he was starving. He reckoned that Tomme had carried him more than a day from the village.

It was infuriating to think that, as he had struggled by boat and foot through one of the densest parts of the rainforest, his own company had a clearance team working so close to his son's new people.

He radioed ahead that he was coming home, and that Uwe Werner was not. Then one of the AmazCo team drove him back along the dirt road in his battered Chevrolet. Markham was greatly relieved when they reached the logging camp, with its primitive amenities, its cold beer and its landing strip. A small plane flew in a few hours later, and by evening he was wearily knocking on the door of his apartment in Belore. He had wanted this first meeting with Jean to be on their own territory, so he had not invited her to meet him.

When she opened the door she nearly died. "My *God*. What's happened to you?"

He was wearing borrowed clothes, which were too short in the arm and leg and too loose elsewhere, so that he had tied the trousers with string. Unshaven and unkempt, his left arm bleeding through the shirt where he had knocked the dressing in the plane, he looked an awful sight.

"I lost my clothes," he said. "Hi, Jean."

He stepped inside and hugged her. She was overwhelmed by his smell and backed off, holding him at arm's length, but holding him; she looked very tired, but very lovely and at that moment what Bill needed most was a long, warm hug. But that was not possible, not until he had said what he needed to say.

Heather came in, jaunty and bright, and was delighted to see her father. "You're back so quickly this time!"

"I had an unfortunate encounter. I lost everything, my clothes, my pack, my gun—"

"And Uwe Werner," Heather said. "Is he dead?"

Bill nodded grimly. He went to the drinks cabinet and poured a very small brandy for himself. Jean stood behind him, refused a drink, just stood, wringing her hands in front of her. Watching. Waiting.

The tension was terrible. He was back far earlier than usual. From Grey's Landing he had radioed that he had heard word of the Smiling People. Uwe Werner was dead, which was catastrophic news.

"You know something, don't you?" Jean asked after a while. Bill drained the brandy, then watched Jean closely. It was so hard to judge what her reaction would be, how she would take the news. Her need to find Tommy was as powerful as his had been, and Bill feared she would not rest, would not settle, would not live again if she knew that he was alive but not coming home.

He had been thinking of how to handle the awful situation, with its tragic irony: that the boy they hoped to rescue had died, although the boy that was their son lived on. Tommy had to be left alone, now. Bill was convinced of that, but he had been there, he had seen Tommy, seen the contentment with which the boy lived his life . . .he had seen him married. He had felt the gulf between them, between their worlds, as real, as unbridgeable as time itself.

And he had worked through his grief in the company of the boy whom he had once loved so much.

Jean would never accept the new status quo. She would *have* to see Tommy for herself. And her heart would break if she heard herself called "ghost mother."

It was an awesome responsibility, this knowledge that he carried.

And he did not feel equal to that responsibility, nor worthy of Jean. But he said what he had decided to say, and though the lie made him die inside, once it was said he was able to think more clearly.

"Jean, little Tommy is dead. I found out. That's why I'm back so quickly."

Jean's face went deathly white. Slowly she shook her head, staring directly at her husband, searching his own face for some sign that he hadn't meant what he had said. "No," she whispered. "No. I don't believe it."

"He's dead, Jean. I'm sorry. I wanted to be able to bring you such—such wonderful news . . . but I can't. I'm desperately sorry."

She turned from him and sat down on the edge of an armchair. Her breathing was ragged, her face a mask of uncertainty and growing grief. Heather's eyes had filled with tears, but she sniffed them back, smiled and sat down by her mother, putting her arms round her.

After a moment Jean became angry. She shook her head more violently.

"Did you see him killed?"

"I didn't say he had been killed," Bill whispered.

"How do you know he's dead?" Jean challenged.

"I was told."

She stood up and came over to him. *She knows*, he thought grimly. *She can tell that I'm lying*.

"Told? What does that mean? Told! Who told you?"

Bill said, "The Indians who took him."

"You found the Smiling People? You made contact?"

He nodded. "Their proper name is the Invisible People. They are very gentle and peace-loving."

"Is that why they abducted Tommy? Because they're peace-loving?'

"I don't know," Bill said. He was hot and itchy, and the lie was burning deeper.

Jean asked, "So they told you he was dead. How did he die? What did they tell you?"

"All they told me was that he died. Does it matter? He's dead. The search is over."

"It *does* matter!" Jean shouted. "And the search *isn't* over. It can't be! How did they treat him? Were they kind to him?"

Bill reached out and took her hand. She tried to tug away, but he held her the harder, pulling her towards him roughly. "They were good people. They know about the white man. They watch us from the edge of the forest. They are hunters and gatherers, but not cannibals. For whatever reason they took him, they looked after him. He had food and warmth and comfort. All they said was that he died. I suppose he fell ill. Perhaps it was an accident. I don't know. I don't *want* to know."

Slowly Jean pulled her hand from her husband's. Tears glistened in her eyes, then began to flow. Still staring at him, she shook her head again. "Bill, I don't believe you. I just don't believe he's dead."

"You mean you don't *want* to believe he's dead."

"I mean I don't believe *you*!"

She turned away from him and walked quickly into the bedroom. Bill felt the room closing in on him. It was stiflingly hot. He walked quickly to the balcony windows, drew them open and stepped out into the cool evening air. He took several deep breaths, his eyes closed, listening to the familiar noise of the city around him.

Heather came out and stood with him. After a while she said, "Mom'll be okay. Just give her a little time to get used to the news."

Bill nodded. "It's not going to be easy for any of us."

Heather said, "I think I understand what you meant . . . when you said *little* Tommy is dead." Bill glanced at her quickly. She went on, "I think I understand what you found. And I think I understand what you must be going through."

Bill reached out for her, cradling her to him. He took a deep breath and let it out very slowly. "Don't say anything."

"Of course not. Not until you're ready."

"It's all over. Goodbye, Belore; goodbye, Brazil. We're going back to the States."

2

They followed the Fierce Ones for many days. It had rapidly become clear that Jacareh was not taking the young women back to his own village. They were heading to the east, and running very fast. They were following the hunt-trails of the old tribes, and soon Wanadi realized where they were going.

When the tracks of the Fierce Ones ended at a river and did not begin again on the other side Tomme was almost distraught.

"Now we will never find them," he said. The young warriors with him were equally upset. They crouched by the river and watched its flow. The memories of their wives were becoming grey with death.

Only Wanadi and Samanpo knew different.

"Make rafts," Wanadi said. "We will follow them down the river."

Tomme said, "From rafts we will never be able to see where they came back to the shore."

With a smile, Wanadi touched his son's cheek. "This is one of the great trails," he said. "Tomme, I have hunted here many times. You too have travelled this hunt-trail."

Puzzled, Tomme said, "When?"

"When you were still a ghost. When we saved you from the wilderness."

Now Tomme understood. "This is the trail that goes to the edge of the World! This is where I ran with you when I came *into* the World."

Which meant that Jacareh and his hunters, and the women of the Invisible People, would have to come to the bank at a certain place. They were following the old trail into the territory that had once been theirs. And Wanadi knew it.

They made their rafts. They plunged into the swirling waters and flowed down-stream. Wanadi and Tomme lay on a raft together, Samanpo and Mapi on another. Their two rafts floated close to the banks, searching for the signs of the Fierce People's beaching. The Fierce People had carried their rafts with them through the jungle, since there was no sign of wood-cutting where their tracks ended at the river.

Samanpo saw the place. It was a broken branch, a small white feather stuck in the break.

Now there followed the struggle to the shore. Wanadi and Tomme ended up a long way down-river and had to trek back to the point where the sign had been.

"One of the women did this," Samanpo said.

All along, there had been the occasional sign from the captured women, marking out the route by which they were being taken. Broken grass, feathers in the bark of trees, broken spider's webs. But Wanadi knew exactly where the trail was leading, and when they had recovered from the river journey they began to run again, pursuing closely.

They came to the edge of the World. They stood in the forest and stared out across the vast waste land. There was not a tree nor a shrub to be seen. And yet the land was alive; it crawled with the great machines that could eat the skin of the World. They did this now, plunging their jaws into the red earth and scooping it up, stripping it down to the bare rock below.

"They are taking the skin off the World," Mapi whispered, horrified. "How will she breathe?"

No one could answer him.

The forest had not been totally destroyed. A tendril of thinned woodland reached out across the wilderness; on one side was the cut earth, on the other a place of scrub and bush, where once the land had been stripped bare and now the forest was growing back.

After a while the thin band of forest widened and became dense again, even though a road cut through it. This was the place that Wanadi remembered from that time, ten hunt-trails in his past, when he had found Tomme. To his astonishment, for he knew the voracious appetites of the Termite People, the edge of the World here was much as it had been then.

But now, as they looked into the wilderness from the concealing growth of forest, they had a shock.

Where there had been a river, now there was just an immense wall of white stone. It was curved and it spanned the river valley. Wanadi had many times in his youth constructed stone dams across small rivers, to create a pool in which fish would gather and could be speared or poisoned easily. Since this stone wall had not been here the last time he had stared into this land, he knew instantly that the Termite People had constructed it. A great water dam, creating a great pool on the other side. Wanadi wondered if the Termite People expected to catch fish the size of their machines in that pool. He chuckled. If they did they would be disappointed. They might catch *more* fish . . . on the other hand, looking at that stone wall, the pool behind it would be so deep that the fish could easily hide at the bottom, and never be seen by the Termite fishermen.

How foolish these ghost people were! If they had only asked people like Wanadi's people, they could have told them the easiest ways to fish. There was no need to make such big blocks in the rivers.

He shook his head. The Termite People were hopeless. They had no idea.

Suddenly Mapi called out. "There! The Fierce People!"

The youth was slung from the lower branches of a tree. Tomme rapidly climbed to the same vantage-point. Distantly, grey shapes against the heat and haze of dust, a line of painted Indians was trotting across the waste land. Among them, bound with vines, were the weary shapes of the women from Wanadi's village.

"Kachiri!" Tomme screamed. He jumped to the ground, falling heavily. He was immediately up and running, but Wanadi shouted at him, "Come back!" Wanadi's voice was so strong, so authoritative, that Tomme stopped and turned, ashamed at his impetuous behaviour.

Wanadi said, "We are not Invisible in the Dead World. You should know this, Tomme."

Tomme said, "If we kill the ones who see us, then we *are* still Invisible."

"If you kill a person, even a ghost, just because he uses his eyes, then you are a ghost yourself. No, Tomme. That is not our way. We will follow them along the edge of the World."

It was not hard to keep the Fierce People in view. For whatever reason Jacareh had taken his band, and the captives, through the open land, it meant that their dust trail could always be seen. And they ran no faster than through the forest, since the heat slowed them badly, and the fear of being seen had them continually ducking and crouching and watching the distant activity of the Termite People.

Even Jacareh, the bold leader of his tribe, was uncomfortable when away from the confines and safety of the trees.

At dusk Wanadi finally led his own small group to the place where their women had been brought. From the undergrowth they stared at the small, square structure, with its lights that shone brightly through the windows in its walls. There was laughter from within, and singing. Jacareh's warriors were seated in a group outside this place, eating food from a wide bowl and drinking from the strange vessels that the Termite People used.

Jacareh, though . . . Jacareh was different.

Wanadi knew at once that Jacareh was aware of the fact that he had been followed. In his jaguar's cape, with his body painted fiercely white and red, he prowled up and down just inside the high fence that surrounded the outpost. He carried the weapon which he had stolen from Tomme's ghost father. Around his neck he wore a necklace on which were hung strange black blocks, their edges gleaming.

"That is the source of the fire," Tomme whispered. "They are the tiny arrows that fly without being seen."

Wanadi led the way cautiously round the outpost, keeping to the concealment of the undergrowth as much as was possible. Four of the women from his village—including his own young wife, Pequi—were huddled in a miserable group on the covered boardwalk of the building. Standing guard over them were two Brazilian traders, each carrying a weapon, each smoking. They were discussing the women, and laughing. One of them kept reaching out to tease and touch Pequi. Wanadi was proud to see how she ignored him. One of the other women hissed and spat like an angry cat.

Between the building and the forest's edge there was a high fence. Strange dead trees ran around that fence, and from their tops were slung black vines. Tomme stared at these and felt uneasy about them, recognizing them from his past. He became very anxious when the young warrior, Marukani, proposed climbing the trees and swinging into the compound by way of the vines.

"I am called the monkey," Marukani said. "I can show you the way."

"No," Tomme said. He stared at the black vines. "They are dangerous. We should not climb them."

Marukani said, "They are just the vines of the Termite People. Let me at least try . . ."

Wanadi nodded. Marukani took his bow and a handful of arrows and tied them about his body. Then he ran quickly to the fence, scaled it with no difficulty and swung out on to the dead trees. He was out of sight of the women, and their guards. The Fierce People continued to sing and drink, and Jacareh himself had joined them.

Marukani had reached the top of the pole. He stretched out and grabbed hold of the nearest vine. Then he swung on it, using two hands. It held his weight. He maneuvered along it, and came over the fence itself. A second vine ran in parallel to the first. The young warrior hesitated for a moment, staring down to the ground, and then decided that he would have a better fall if he moved to the second vine.

As he touched it he screamed. Blue fire played around his hands. His body danced on the vine, like a monkey poisoned with *curicaro*, like a dancer in the dreamlight.

And then flames swathed his arms, and he fell to the ground and lay still, except for the twitching that could so often accompany the dead.

All of the watchers were shocked into silence, paralyzed with fear and incomprehension. Then Wanadi led the way back into the forest, back into deep cover. All went except for Tomme, who stayed to see what would happen.

The two guards had heard Marukani's scream. They ran round the building and kicked at the body, calling out in their wilderness tongue. Another man came. He was shorter and fatter. He carried one of the small guns, like ghost father had carried.

Tomme watched this man pick up two of Marukani's arrows.

"Jacareh!" he called sharply. "Jacareh!"

The leader of the Fierce People appeared. His gun was cradled round his neck. He was chewing some meat; the red paint around his mouth, in the white mask, made him look hideous, like an insect.

He laughed when he saw the arrows. They all looked out through the fence, almost directly to where Tomme was crouched, watching.

Tomme returned to the others.

"Jacareh knows who we are. They will come searching for us."

Wanadi's voice was hushed in the darkness and stillness of their hiding place. "We must attack."

Samanpo disagreed. "If we attack now we will all die. They all have the weapons of the wilderness."

"Without our women we are dead anyway," Wanadi reminded him. "Without our wives we are a people with no future. We will become grey shadows in the forest. No. We must attack."

"Listen!" Tomme said suddenly.

Distant, but getting closer, was the hissing of the Fierce People.

They were running in single file, as always, weaving and winding their way to where Wanadi's hunters were crouched. The Invisible People immediately melted back into the undergrowth, spreading out in a wide arc.

Then Jacareh's voice taunted them, shouted loud above the hissing of his warriors. "You are not Invisible! You are not Invisible! We can see you like logs on the water . . ."

And as he shouted he let off the fire from his weapon. The forest screamed with the noise of the invisible arrows. Only they were not invisible, this time; they glowed as they streaked into the trees and bush. They seemed to light up the faces of the Invisible People. Mapi yelled, close to Tomme, and bolted back through the forest. His cousin, Onatu, ran as well, and the yellow fire struck him in the back. He was lifted from the ground and flung against the trunk of a tree. Tomme smelled blood.

"We must run!" Tomme shouted. Yellow fire hissed above him and exploded against a tree. He ducked and pulled away. The Fierce People were shooting real arrows too, and were standing in plain sight, not worried about keeping cover.

Wanadi called back, "Too old to run. Uluru has whispered to me . . ."

"No, father!"

But Tommie's pleading cry was not heeded. Wanadi appeared from cover and rushed at Jacareh. Jacareh whooped with delight. He pointed the gun at the leader of the Invisible People and bright fire struck the old man in the chest, flinging him backwards, throwing him to the ground. Wanadi's arrow, drawn and ready, was loosed as he was struck, and the weapon, coated with poison, seared through Jacareh's arm. The man grunted and quickly pulled the arrow through. Still trying to shoot his gun, he raised his arm to his lips and sucked furiously, trying to get the poison out.

Tomme was frantic. Wanadi was struggling on the ground, arms raised, desperately trying to nock a second arrow. Tomme ran for him. As he ran he fired at Jacareh, and the leader of the Fierce People knocked the arrow aside with almost arrogant ease. He pointed the gun at Tomme, but no fire came, even though he shook it violently.

"Father!" Tomme shouted, and began to drag Wanadi back to cover. A Fierce One leapt at him, bow drawn, and Tomme flung his spear. The man was impaled on the point and backed away screaming. Tomme nocked an arrow and shot another warrior through the neck. An arrow glanced off his face, a warrior ran at him with a spear . . .

Mapi was there, suddenly, violently impaling the Fierce One with his own spear. He helped Tomme lift the wounded old man on to his son's back, and Tomme staggered into the darkness, Mapi behind him keeping the hunters at bay.

Soon the sound of Jacareh and his men had stopped. They had gone back to the wilderness enclosure to feast some more, and to drink, and to brag their great victory. Three of them had been killed, but Jacareh would survive the arm wound, and Jacareh was the true source of evil in the village of the Fierce People.

Tomme could understand what had happened. His ghost father had lost the gun and Jacareh had found it. But it had had no fire. He had traded with the wilderness people for fire: the price, the women of the Invisible People, for use as slaves no doubt.

But these thoughts were secondary, for the moment. Wanadi, his father and the leader of the village, was dying.

"Put me down, son," the old man said.

"I must get you to water and to safety," Tomme said, staggering under the weight, still pushing on through the forest behind Samanpo and the others.

Wanadi gasped and groaned. The warmth of his blood on Tomme's back was spreading.

"Son, I must die. Put me down. This is not dignified. Let me die watching the stars."

Ahead of them Tomme heard water, the small stream they had crossed earlier. Following Samanpo, he waded through the stream and on to the bank, then carefully walked backwards through his own footprints, as the others had already done. Then he splashed up-stream for a way, and was helped ashore at the rocks. It was a simple trick, but if any of Jacareh's hunters should follow them, it might work to throw them off the trail.

So at last Wanadi found his dignity.

Mapi helped him from Tomme's back, and they laid him down in a cradle of leaves and twigs, crossing his arms on his chest and covering him with warm moss. Above them the sky was dark with swirling rain clouds, but in between a few stars could be seen and they shone in Wanadi's eyes as he watched them.

After a while the old man's breathing became more peaceful. The sound of the stream was like a gentle voice, calling him. It was the only sound in the forest.

"Where is Samanpo?" Wanadi whispered.

"I'm here."

Samanpo reached out and rested a hand on Wanadi's forehead.

"Brother, when you are home, and the village is built again, set free my soul with fire and add a few grains of my bones to the ancestral dust."

"I will. I will make sure it is done."

"Thank you . . ."

He moved his head a little and saw Tomme. Tomme placed his hand on his father's face. Wanadi said, "Well, Tomme, now it is up to you to do what I could not do. Rescue our people. Make us whole again."

"I will, father. I know exactly what I must do."

Wanadi smiled. Already the gleam of the stars was beginning to fade from his eyes. "One day this will be a great story to tell. Don't forget to include me—"

"I shan't . . ."

There was movement by the small river. Tomme glanced towards it and saw a sinuous shape sliding into the water. It splashed for a moment, breaking the waves, before gliding away up-stream.

Wanadi had once told his son that when a great hunter dies the Anaconda herself comes to carry away the spirit. When the snake had gone Tomme turned back to his father.

The old man's eyes were open, and he was smiling, but there was no life left in him.

Tomme wasted no time. There was no time to waste. He stood up and gathered his weapons. To Samanpo he said, "Uncle, do as my father said. Take his body home and wait for me."

Samanpo nodded. The rest of the Invisible People—five only out of all the village—came out of the forest and knelt by their dead chief. All but Mapi. Mapi clutched his bow and arrows, and he stood with Tomme. Whatever Tomme was about to do, they would do it together.

Samanpo said, "How will you get back our women?"

"I will go even further beyond the edge of the World," Tomme said. "I will find my ghost father again. He knows about the bright fire, about the wilderness weapons. I will ask him to help us."

Samanpo nodded. He and another hunter reached down to pick up Wanadi's body. Tomme and Mapi ran swiftly along the edge of the river, crossed it, and were soon lost from sight.

3

That journey into the Dead World was the most terrifying time that Tomme had ever endured. He was more relieved than he would admit that Mapi was with him. It was always easy to find courage when you were in company.

For all of the first day they ran along the straight road through the forest, terrified by the great lumbering machines that roared past them as they cowered in hiding, waiting for all sound to disappear before venturing back into the open. Mapi was deeply distressed to see the great trees that were being hauled into "graveyards," there to be cut and dismembered. The whine of the teeth that cut the trees sounded, to him, like a wailing cry of distress.

On the second day they found a field of mango trees. The trees had been planted along the flight of an arrow, and the ground between them was bare. But the fruit tasted good, and they gorged themselves contentedly. The only shock came as they rested in this unnatural forest. A machine appeared above them, suddenly, terrifyingly, its roar like the machines on the road. From its tail there flowed a plume of white dust, which was cloying and choking as it settled on the scampering Indians.

They continued to follow the road, and soon their bodies were the color of the red earth, and they were invisible again, since they could conceal themselves by lying flat. The sounds, and the great machines, were less terrifying now, less startling, even if they remained confusing. At times the forest that bordered the road was burning. Wilderness men stood and watched the flames, or moved through the blackened remains of the World cutting down the stumps.

On the third day, though, they reached the end of the road. It stopped quite suddenly at the edge of a great river. Across the river was the Dead Forest, the place from Tomme's dreams, the high stone huts and crowded places where the Termite People lived as their name implied—like ants, shoulder to shoulder in tiny passages.

Mapi was overwhelmed by the vastness of the city. The two of them ran, at a crouch, down to the river's edge where there was a concealing stand of reeds. The dust washed off their bodies and they became visible again.

"How do we get across?" Mapi murmured. The river was far too wide to swim; there were vast ships, belching smoke, passing up and down, ships big enough to smash whole trees, let alone small human bodies.

"We must find a canoe," Tomme said. "My ghost father lives in that place, somewhere. We have to go there."

They crawled through the reeds. There were several canoes on the water line, but they were all wrecked. At last they saw a shanty hut. An old Indian, wearing the clothes of the wilderness, was sleeping in a chair outside it. A canoe with a solid hull was moored among the reeds close by.

Mapi slipped the mooring rope, and Tomme pushed the boat out into the water. When they were well off-shore they clambered into it. The shirt Indian woke and shouted at them, throwing stones into the river.

"He saw us and we didn't kill him," Mapi whispered. "What have we become, Tomme? We are no longer the Invisible People."

"Perhaps we aren't. Not until the women are rescued, and we are back in the World. This is a terrible place, Mapi, with terrible creatures, and frightening ghosts. We cannot expect to come into the dark Otherworld and behave as if we were on a simple hunting trip."

Mapi paddled frantically out across the water. "I hope you're right," he said.

The current took them and spun them round. They straightened up again and paddled on. The water was thick with a gleaming, sticky substance. Plants and bits of wilderness rubbish bobbed on the sluggish waves, and Mapi gathered what he could, hoping to learn something about the ghosts into whose realm he had ventured.

Soon they could see that the water's edge was hidden below huts built on stilts, that stretched a long way out across the river. Smoke rose from the roofs of many of these, and from them too came wonderful smells of cooking. Smoked meats. Fish. The sweet smell of vegetables in water.

Mapi was always hungry. He stopped paddling, tilted his head back, and breathed deeply. "These ghosts aren't so bad," he said.

Tomme said, "Stop thinking of your stomach and help us into cover."

They glided below the stilt-huts, pulling themselves to the shore by using the rotting wood of the props. Above them, voices shouted and laughed, children ran, and dogs barked.

Tying the canoe carefully to one of the stilts, they dropped into the water and waded ashore to what appeared to be a ramshackle landing platform, a bridge of wood half submerged. This led them to a winding alley, lined on all sides by cold hard walls. There were a few windows covered with colored rags. The whole alley shook and swayed as they walked cautiously through the labyrinth of passages. All around them they could hear the sounds of the people who lived there, their voices, their movement, but they could see none of them.

And then suddenly a voice hailed them. Startled, they swung round, trying to nock arrows to their bows, but in this narrow space they just succeeded in tangling their bows together.

A man stood in the narrow crack of a doorway. From behind him came cooking smells. He was dressed in trousers and a baggy shirt, but he was an Indian, and still had skin-cuts on his face which neither Tomme nor Mapi recognized.

"I know you," the man said in their own language. "You are the Invisible People."

Mapi was frightened. All his life he had been taught that if he was ever seen his spirit would not find rest in the dreamlight. But now he was too frozen to react.

The man gestured to them. They walked slowly forward, then followed him into the dark hut-space.

"Don't be afraid," the man said. "If you stay in the alley like that someone will see you and shoot fire at you."

Tomme and Mapi crouched by the wall. Slowly their eyes accustomed to the gloom. Two men of their own age were sitting in the hut, and an old woman. They all smiled. The old woman was stirring a large pot of broth, and there were chunks of a strange-looking bread on a wooden plate.

"How do you know us?" Tomme asked.

"By your arrows," the man said. "And by the green on your face. It sparkles. It is the Light of the Forest."

"Then who are you that you can know about us?"

"We were once a part of the World," the old man said. "We lived out there, not far from you. We hunted at night and you called us the Bat People."

Tomme gasped. The Bat People had disappeared from the World many hunt-trails in the past, but Wanadi had told stories of them. No wonder Tomme had not recognized the skin-cuts.

"My name in this place is Carlos. These are my sons. In this place we wear shirts, and we are called shirt Indians. These huts are our village, now, and no one else can live here. But it is not the same. When we were in the World we would drink the magic drink and fly above the forest to the House of Thunder. There we would talk to our ancestors."

Tomme had a small gourd of cocassa tied to his loincloth. He patted it. "If you help us, perhaps you will fly again."

Carlos nodded slowly. "Here there are also many magic drinks," he said wistfully. "You fly a little and fall into your own filth. Soon you fall further and drown in the river. And then there is work for one more Indian."

Mapi asked, "Why don't you go back to the World? Why do you stay in this terrible place?"

"Because we wear the shirts of the white men," Carlos said. "When the shirt has been put upon you it grows below your skin, and you can only take it off for a few minutes, just to wash it. Besides," he said, "the true edge of the World is so far away from us, now, I don't think we could ever reach it again."

Tomme patted his chest. "But we have just come from there. It is a terrifying journey, but we are here, and we will be going back. You should come with us."

Carlos stared at him. He said something in a strange tongue and the two younger men murmured. The old woman laughed, then began to dish out the soup into hard, cold bowls.

"My sons were born here," Carlos said. "But they dream of the World."

Mapi reached for the bowl that was proffered, and nodded his thanks gratefully. Tomme refused to eat. No one insisted that he should. While Mapi abated his awesome appetite, Tomme asked Carlos for help.

"We seek my ghost father. His name is Bill. We need his help to free our wives, who have been captured by the white men."

Carlos shook his head. "Bill? I have heard that name many times, many different people. If your ghost father lives in the city he will have another name—"

"Then I don't know it."

Mapi had finished eating. "We can disguise ourselves as ghosts and hunt through the big village. If we call loudly enough he will hear us."

Carlos laughed. "This big village stretches into the sky as well. You could search it for ten hunt-trails and never find one man called Bill."

Tomme suddenly felt an overwhelming hopelessness. They sat in silence for a while. Around them, the shanty town came more noisily to life as the afternoon light waned and dusk approached.

Then Tomme came to a decision. "I must call the eagle," he said. "I must look through the dreamlight at the past, to when I was truly a Termite Child."

Carlos frowned. "You were once . . . ?" he leaned forward, then gasped as for the first time he recognized that Tomme's features had not been painted; he *was* yellow-haired; his skin *was* pale below the water-streaked green paint.

Carlos and his two sons—who were called Paulo and Rico—led the way to an open area of waste ground, screened by trees and yet in full sight of the tall, brightly lit structures of the city. There they all sat down, save Tomme, who remained standing and with his arms outstretched. He stared into the dusk sky for a long time then slowly lowered his arms.

After a while a dark bird wheeled across the grey clouds, a majestic silhouette, hovering above them. Carlos stared into the heavens with amazement. "It *is* an eagle," he said in hushed tones. "I have never seen one this close to the city before."

Tomme dropped to a crouch. Mapi had loaded a short piece of bamboo pipe with a small pinch of the cocassa. Tomme held the end of the pipe to his nostril. Mapi blew quickly, and the drug blasted into Tomme's system . . .

The wind took him. He felt its gentle fingers carry his body higher. The

Light of the World changed from dusk's grey gloom to the green of the dreamlight. He sailed rapidly across the great city, and the wind tugged him down, then pushed him to the right, and he whirled and wheeled and . . .

. . . reached out his wings. Struck hard against the air, felt his body soar, struck again and turned to watch the city below. He feathered and fell, beat his wings hard and levelled off, skimming the rooftops, circling the wide tracks and clearings below where the lights of the city moved like men with torches.

Then ahead of him was a great stone tree; and hearth spaces had been carved into the tree, and light gleamed in them. He flew towards the highest of these rooms, and in the shimmering green light of this ghostly realm he saw two children, standing on a balcony. They were watching him. The boy was pointing. The girl, who was younger, was clapping her hands together; the smile on her face was one of absolute delight.

He swooped low across them, circled once more, then beat his wings hard and began to fly towards the forest.

The face of the boy was like a face out of his dreams. His own face, full of innocence, yet somehow shadowed, as if he were already aware that he was a spirit from the World, trapped in the wilderness.

He awoke with a sudden shock. He struggled, but Mapi held his arms. After a moment he remembered where he was, and he lay back, breathing hard and fast.

Then he smiled. Carlos leaned close. Mapi too.

"What did you see?" Mapi asked.

"Everything I need to see," Tomme said, still breathless. "It was wonderful. I flew high above the great village. There are so many lights! And I saw where I lived. I remembered the place, and it was shown to me out of my dreams."

He sat up and shook his head, then pinched his nostrils to dry them.

"I must go there now. You wait for me here. I shall go and fetch ghost father."

He ran quickly through the city, no longer afraid. He kept to the shadows, a shadow himself, a darting shape, invisible to eyes that were not trained to see him.

At last he came to the playground. For a moment he stood, half in, half out of the tall, lush green vegetation that grew at its edge. There were no children playing here now, but in his mind, in his dreams, he could see dusky-skinned children swinging on the bars and crawling over the strange structures. He could hear laughter and taunting. The place filled him with memories of sadness, of being alone.

Quickly, then, he passed across the open area. He came to the base of the great building, the stone tree with its gleaming hearths carved into its side.

With his bow and arrows securely strapped across his back he hauled himself on to the surrounding fence, then leaped to the wall and found finger- and toe-grips between the blocks of stone that made up the trunk. He eased his way upwards until he reached the first balcony. From there his climb was simple.

Within a few minutes he was standing on the balcony at the top of the building. He approached the hearth space and found it protected by a wall of hard water; *glass*, he remembered. He stepped forward and peered into the light of the interior.

His ghost father sat at a table. Next to him was a woman, and Tomme remembered her immediately. "Mum-mee," he whispered to himself. He was amazed again at seeing these people who, for so long, had been just dreams to him.

Ghost mother and ghost father were looking at small pieces of colored paper. Sometimes they laughed, and sometimes they looked sad. Tomme watched them for a while, then reached out and tapped his fingers on the glass.

4

They had been intending to begin packing that evening. In two days the family would fly back to the United States. New jobs waited for them. And a new school for Heather. It had all been arranged with AmazCo's usual efficiency.

The Markhams' time in Brazil was done.

Inevitably, as Bill and Jean began to stack up books ready for the boxes, they found their old photograph albums, and could not resist a nostalgic turn through the pages.

In the days since Bill's return, Jean had come more to terms with her husband's insistence that Tommy was dead, and that the searching—for him at least—was over. A part of her was as glad as Bill that at last they could return to a more normal life. Yes, there would be the doubt in her, the feeling of having been betrayed; but she had chosen not to think about the nature or detail of that betrayal. She had experienced enough hurt as it was.

And so had Bill. She knew that quite clearly. And she was now resigned to the fact that it was time to go home.

They had just opened the second album, and were remembering their holiday in Ireland—Tommy had been just four—when someone tapped on the window. They looked up, and for a moment sat utterly still.

Outside the window the ghost tapped on the glass again. Then he raised a hand and leaned close, pressing his nose against the glass. His face was like a halloween mask, striped with green and black, his eyes wide, his mouth moving silently.

"Oh my God . . ." Bill Markham whispered.

"What is it?" Jean said. "Who is it?"

Bill looked at her quickly. She caught his gaze, saw the pain in his eyes, recognized the reason for his inability to speak. She turned back to the ghastly grey figure at the window, and suddenly—

"Tommy! My God, it's Tommy!"

In the other room, hearing her mother's words, Heather screamed. She came running through into the sitting-room. When she saw Tommy she stood absolutely still, her face registering her own private shock.

Jean had run to the balcony window and wrenched it open. The warm night air blew in against her. She stood, shaking her head slowly, staring at the tall young man outside. The more she looked at him the more she recognized of the Tommy she remembered so well.

"Tommy," she whispered again, and reached out a hand to him, touching his shoulder, then his cheek, then the long earrings he wore. "I knew you were alive. I knew you'd find us again, one day."

"Mum-mee," Tomme said, recognizing her from his dreams. He smiled at her, but drew away as if uncomfortable at her proximity. Then Bill came up and ushered him into the sitting-room, sliding the balcony window closed.

"Tomme," he said, and then spoke in Tupi. Tomme at once responded, telling him urgently how, when they had returned to the village, they had found it burning and their young women abducted. Among them Caya, whom he had liked so much, and Kachiri. They needed help. They were strong in their World, but in the wilderness they could not hope to stand against the white man's weapons. And Jacareh, leader of the Fierce People, had a *gun*, and had killed many of the Invisible People with it.

Bill was shocked. He remembered all too clearly the way Jacareh had waved his own weapon at him, as the current of the river had swept him and Tomme away. And Jacareh would have found the remaining clips of bullets in the white man's pack on returning to the village.

Knowing Jacareh, as Bill now felt he did, the hunter would have exhausted the clips fast. Too fast. To get more, then, he had almost certainly contacted white traders.

In exchange for ammunition these traders had wanted women for prostitution. And Jacareh had known just where to get them.

Jean had been listening to Tomme's frantic speech. Heather had given her brother a huge squeeze, which he had not taken well. He was anxious and upset, and he seemed to be saying, I have no time for frivolity.

Jean sat down and motioned that Tomme should do the same. She was suddenly slightly disturbed that he was so blatantly naked. His loincloth was more functional as a belt than as a modest covering. Tomme glanced apprehensively at his father, who said something to him. Tomme smiled and sat next to his mother. Then he kept talking. Heather sat on the arm of the chair and began to examine the wild young man minutely.

"He could do with a bath," she said. "Very definitely. Look at his earrings, though. Aren't they gorgeous?" She touched the colored discs of bone that dangled from his ears.

Jean said, "Tommy . . . Everything is going to be all right, now. Do you understand? Everything. All. Right." Even as she spoke the words she knew that the sentiments were empty, meaningless to her son. She spoke them because she *needed* to speak them, she needed to indulge the delusion of the boy's triumphant rediscovery—it was part of accepting the terrible fact that he had moved beyond her. It was a part of grief.

Tomme stared at her blankly. Then he smiled and whispered a few words to her. Jean was delighted at the communication. She looked at Bill. "What was that?"

"He says that his ghost mother is very beautiful, like his real mother."

Jean frowned. "Who is his ghost mother?"

"You are."

"I'm his *real* mother!" she said, upset.

"His real mother is Uluru," Bill said. "But she's dead now. He has drunk the ash of her bones, and she will always live inside him."

"Great!" Heather said enthusiastically, her eyes glowing. "Ask him lots more things like that. Especially about sex. No one knows about their sex lives."

"Heather!" Jean protested. "This is your brother."

"Brothers can have sex lives too," Heather said, with a quick smile at her father.

Jean looked back at Bill. And suddenly she, too, saw the funny side. Slowly she smiled. She shook her head and said sadly, "He doesn't remember me, does he?"

"Yes he does," Bill said. "To him, you are ghost mother, and dearly loved by him. He dreams of you. When he's dead you and he—me too—we'll all be reunited in the dreamlight. That's their otherworld, where they exist both as themselves and as their animal counterpart."

Heather ran from the room, saying, "Oh God, this is too good to miss." She returned with a tape-recorder, and set it running. Tomme watched the small cassette turning. Jean said to him, "Tommy. I am so glad that you are home. I am glad that you have found us. If you want, now, you can live with us again, as we used to." She spoke slowly, and used her smattering of Tupi, but Tomme just watched her blankly. Bill felt very uncomfortable. He knew the true reason why Tomme was here, and he knew how futile any attempt to keep him in Belore would be, and he recognized too that Jean did not yet comprehend how this youth, though her son, was *not* her son. It had taken Bill himself a long while to accept the sad truth. Now, at last, Jean's time of grieving could really begin, and there would be no need for more lies between them.

"Honey," he said to Heather, "show Tomme round the apartment. Show him a few things from his old room."

Heather nodded quickly. When Bill suggested to the young man that he might go and explore the "stone tree," Tomme reluctantly went.

Jean watched him go. The moment he was out of the room she let her anger express itself. "How could you do this to me? After all we've been through together! How could you *lie* to me, Bill? What a despicable thing to do!"

"I didn't know how to tell you," he said quietly. "I didn't know *what* to tell you. The Tommy we've been looking for *is* dead. You've got to accept that, Jean."

Furious, she swung on him. "*That's* Tommy! In there. Naked. Filthy. Primitive. Stinking . . . but that's Tommy! *Our* Tommy. Our son, for Christ's sake. The boy we lost. He's been looking for us. He's found us again. And now we can save him."

"Save him from what?"

She didn't understand how Bill could miss her point. She said, "He has a chance again. It won't take him long to learn the language he's forgotten, to learn our ways again. He may be half Indian, but he's still half Markham. He belongs with us, now. He always has."

Bill shook his head. "That's how I felt too. Until I found him again. I'm surprised that you can't understand the futility of what you're saying." He had begun to sound bitter. "You were always the one with the compassion for the Indians, with nature. Now, suddenly, it's *primitive*. It's *filthy*. It's *stinking*. Is that what you really think of the Indian tribes, Jean?"

"No," she said, shocked by his quiet anger with her. "Of course not. I didn't mean to associate Tommy's state with the culture. You know I didn't."

"I don't know anything of the sort anymore."

She came over to him, eyes wide and moist with tears. She gripped him by the shoulders and shook him. "Listen to me, Bill. He has been well looked after by the Indians. I can see that. And he probably thinks of himself as one of them. I would expect that too. But he doesn't *belong* there. He belongs *here*. *Something* made him come and find us, for God's sake! He didn't just walk out of the forest for nothing. And anyway, in ten years there won't *be* any Indian tribes left. They're being wiped out bit by bit, tribe by tribe, destroyed like pests! Do you want your own son to be part of that extinction?"

Slowly Bill nodded. "I'm not saying that I want that extinction," he said. "But if it's to be that way, then as far as I'm concerned Tomme must be a part of it."

Jean shook her head, her face showing the pain she was feeling. "Listen to you," she breathed. "Your own son."

"*Wanadi's son!*" Bill retorted sharply. "Uluru's son. A hunter from the rainforest. Our ghost son, Jean. The Invisible People drink the ashes of the dead to keep them with them always. We don't have to do that. We had Tommy for seven years. What I value now is those seven years we had, not the years we've missed."

"He *belongs* here, Bill. He can be *made* to belong here. He's only *part* Indian!"

"I understand how you can feel that way, Jean. But you're wrong. There is a power in that forest, and it has called Tommy home to it. Tommy belongs there, now. He is *Tomme*. And as his dead father's son, he is now chief of the Invisible People. He doesn't belong with us anymore. It would astonish him to hear you say that he does. In any case, that's not the reason for his journey."

Jean pulled away, staring at her husband, her face as white as the ashes of the dead. "Then why is he here?"

Briefly, Bill explained what Tomme had told him. Jean remained impassive and cold as he spoke, reacting only when he told her of Tomme's new bride.

"He's *married*?"

"A real beauty. Kachiri. I've never seen so happy a couple. I was there for their wedding, and for the feast. Under Tomme's leadership—under Tomme and *Kachiri's* leadership," he corrected himself, "the Invisible People will soon become great again."

Jean backed away from him and sat down on the arm of the sofa. "Married," she whispered. "Our little Tommy . . ."

"Kachiri has been taken by slavers," Bill said. "That's why Tommy is here. He needs my help."

"Oh my God," Jean murmured. It was coming home to her, rapidly and brutally, what distance there now existed between her and her son. "Tell me everything."

When Bill had finished, Jean was silent for a long while. Her breathing was steady, her eyes dry.

Then she stood again, came over to her husband and took his hand.

"I still think we should try and get him to come back to us."

"It won't work."

She shook her head. Slowly, she said, "You know the one thing I've learned from the last ten years? From all our study? From what we've asked, all that we've discovered? I've learned that the Indians of the Amazon don't have a hope in hell of surviving. We'll destroy them with everything we've got, from measles to tourism. They're creatures in a cage, and we're cutting the cage smaller every day, so that we can see them and marvel at them, and in ten years' time Tommy will be a shirt Indian, poisoned with alcohol, living in a hut made out of tin and cardboard. To the 'white folk' he'll be garbage. Bill, we can save him from that."

"The Indians aren't the only creatures in the cage," Bill said. "Maybe we should work on keeping the cage intact. Tommy has just told me that his father, Wanadi, is dead. He died with great dignity. I think Tommy has been set the best of examples by that old man, and Tommy won't let his people become 'garbage.' "

"They'll die, though."

Bill nodded grimly. "I know they will. I agree with you, Jean. They haven't a hope in hell. In ten years, maybe less . . . yes, the Invisible People will be dust."

"I can't bear to think of it," Jean said.

"Me neither. Then again, maybe they *will* survive. Maybe something will happen that will let them remain invisible." Jean wrapped her arms around her body and turned away from him, saying nothing. Bill added, "Anyway, the choice must be Tommy's."

Before Jean could respond further, Tomme and Heather came out of Tomme's old room. The young man held a plastic rifle. He looked solemnly at his ghost parents and waved the toy weapon towards them. "Gun," he said in English. "Tomme need. Tomme and ghost father must go!"

Tomme was restless, impatient to leave this Dead World, as he called it, and go to where Kachiri and the others were held prisoner. He couldn't understand why his ghost father didn't immediately come with him. And yet, he sensed the sadness in his ghost mother.

So he sat quietly with the family that had once been his, and let Heather make him a pancake—little Tommy's favorite food. The pancake was good. He ate it gratefully, then rose to his feet. He said to Bill, "Can we go now?"

Bill said, "Just a little while more, Tomme. Please. This is the last time we will all be together. And we have waited so long for this."

They turned the pages of the photograph albums, trying to prompt Tomme to remember the happy and hilarious scenes from his early childhood. Birthdays, holidays, Christmas in California, his kindergarten friends, the old dog, Smokie, to whom Tommy had been very attached . . . none of them evoked the slightest response from the young Indian. Jean tried very carefully to make him remember something, anything, but he just watched his ghost mother, more interested in her than in the spirit-images in the book.

For Tomme to be able to make a choice between worlds, he would have to remember the ghost world, he would have to know what options were available to him. But he had forgotten his childhood; he was not looking to choose; availability of options was a Western concept, and no longer appropriate to the Markhams' eldest child. It was a battle for his soul that was lost before it was even fought. It had been lost ten years ago. Just *looking* at Tomme, now, it was clear how far away from the family he had grown.

They sat in their apartment; warm, cosy; Tomme was shaking with apprehension. He was sitting in hell, in the wilderness, in a cave in a stone tree. He was being entertained by ghosts, and he wanted to go.

The album was closed. Bill and Jean exchanged a mutually moist-eyed look. Jean smiled and shrugged. *We tried.*

Bill said, in Tupi, "I'm ready to go, now. I'm ready to help."

But Tomme watched him for a long, thoughtful moment, then glanced at Jean. He seemed immediately to understand the depth of her sadness; perhaps, too, he was intuiting the difficulty she was having in letting go for the last time.

He walked over to her and crouched by her. He whispered something in her ear. She frowned. Through her tearful gaze she looked at him. "I don't understand," she said, almost inaudibly.

Tomme said—Bill translating—"Ghost mother, there is a love in your heart that is trapped. It must be released, so that I can take it with me."

He stood and went to the balcony window, sliding it open a little and making a quick motion with his hand. Bill didn't see what his son had done, although he would soon be able to guess.

Tomme returned. He sat next to Jean again and gently rested his head on her breast, listening to her heart. She stroked his hair quickly, smiling through her tears. "What's he doing?" she asked Bill.

"I don't know."

Tomme said, "I can hear it in there, fluttering. I must release it, then you too will be released."

And he pulled back his ghost mother's blouse and pressed his lips to her breast, sucking fiercely and hard on the skin. Jean was shocked, then perplexed. Tomme kept sucking hard over her heart, then raised his head and opened his mouth.

A brilliant green moth flew out between his lips. He caught it in his hand and cradled it gently. Then he placed it in the pouch at his waist and grinned at Jean.

Jean stared at him for a moment, then laughed, shaking her head. She cradled his head in her hands, and Tomme said, "Now I can take your heart with me, back to my home. Thank you, ghost mother, for the gift."

"You clever so-and-so," she said softly.

She let Tomme go. The young man stood and gathered his weapons. He stood before his sister, tall and proud, a hunter again. He removed his bone earrings and gave them to her. Heather was delighted. Never one to miss an opportunity, she reached out and plucked two of the feathers from his hair.

Jean fetched a camera. She fixed it to timed flash, placed it on the sideboard, and gathered her family round her.

When the flash went off it startled Tomme slightly, but the Markhams had their proof, now, that in one way their dream had come true.

5

The Fierce Hunters were all drunk. Jacareh himself lay curled up in the scoop of a bulldozer, his M16 across his chest, and a bottle held limply in his hand. He snored loudly. His body was painted in the exquisite and grotesque patterns of his tribe, and this, the sign of his one-time magnificence, made him look the sadder.

Markham waited for Tomme and the others to return from their quiet scout around the brothel. The building was a ramshackle collection of shanty huts, strung together with corrugated iron passageways. He had seen many places like it. There would be a large bar, a gambling room, and ten or fifteen disgusting chambers where the girls would take their clients. It was a place used by loggers and traders, mostly, and was a certain way to get diseased. The girls who worked there, often against their will, like Kachiri and the rest of the women of the Invisible People, did not live long.

A group of loggers were outside the main door, drinking from bottles and throwing dice on to the dirt floor. A man with a shotgun lounged there too, watching the forest warily.

When the three Bat People returned, Jabuti—who had once been Carlos—reported that there was a back way from the building. His two sons were even now cutting through the wire fencing at a place where none of the guards could see.

"Good," Markham said. He looked at Jabuti. "Now you are the Bat People again. But will you usc guns?"

Jabuti nodded. "For this one last time . . . yes."

Markham passed him a shotgun. His sons already had automatic pistols.

"Now it begins," Markham said. "Give me five minutes. Then Tomme must utter his war cry. Before that, kill the guards in silence."

Tomme nodded, holding up his blow-pipe. Mapi growled, his eyes glowing at the thought of the fight.

From the number of cars parked outside the building, Markham had guessed that there would be only eight or ten men inside. He was taken by surprise to find that the place was packed. The guard on the door gave him a long, hard look as he walked up. He searched thoroughly, nodded him on through. Inside, he moved through the haze of smoke and light, towards the bar. He ordered a drink and asked about the girls. The barman grinned and pointed across the room. An old woman was parading several girls in front of the ranks of staring men. Bill could see Pequi and Caya, both dressed in alluring skirts and loose blouses that seemed utterly out of place upon them.

He walked over. When Caya was presented he stepped forward and waved his money. The old woman took the money and counted it. Caya was trembling badly, but when she looked at Markham she recognized him. He quickly placed a finger to his lips and she briefly nodded her understanding.

The money was good. Caya stepped down from the stage and Markham took her by the arm. Quickly he explained that, at the sound of Tomme's cry, all the girls should run. And if they were with a man, they would have to disable that man first. There would only be one chance.

Caya led Markham through a curtain to a long, narrow corridor, off which the rooms opened. As she walked she spoke in Tupi so that the other girls would hear and understand. The men with them would not.

Only Pequi was unaware of the plan.

Markham walked straight out through the back door and pushed Caya towards the hole in the fence, where a dim shape in the jungle's edge was beckoning. She ran like a hare, and had vanished in seconds. Markham went back through the brothel and into the bar area.

Pequi was still up on the stage, shivering with fright.

Tomme's war cry was a piercing, grotesque ululation. Markham only just heard it in the noisy bar. At once there were male screams of pain and rage from beyond the curtain. The old woman on the stage looked confused for a moment, then shouted something in Portuguese, and four or five men ran across the bar room, grabbing for weapons.

There was a handgun behind the bar. Markham grabbed for it and shot at the lights. He shouted to Pequi, who saw him and jumped from the stage. He weaved his way through the sudden confusion towards her. The old woman grabbed for a gun, a pistol that was lying on the piano.

She screamed abuse at Markham, who fired above her head, making her duck. Then she swung the pistol round and pulled the trigger. Pequi was thrown against him, and sank limply in his arms, her eyes closed, blood staining her.

With no further thought, Markham leaped through the front of the building. The guard who had been stnding there was still upright against the door frame, but was quite dead. A feathered dart protruded from his neck. The dice-players scattered as Markham fired into the middle of their game. He backed quickly away through the gate, running swiftly into the jungle.

All but Pequi, then, had escaped. Tomme and Kachiri were violently hugging in the small clearing that had been chosen as their rendezvous. The women quickly stripped the white man's clothes from their bodies, until again they were naked, and now, once more, they looked and felt like people.

The Bat People and Markham spread out to cover the retreat into the forest of the hunters. They fired quick bursts at anyone who moved, discouraging them from following. Two men came running through the gate, shrieking angrily. Both were almost naked, and both were limping badly. They waved shotguns and the blast and fire from them sent cascades of leaves and twigs down upon the crouched figures at the jungle's edge.

Then Jacareh appeared. He was sleepy and unsteady. He peered at the forest, then shouted to his drunken hunters. They stirred and stood, gathering their weapons.

They came in pursuit.

Markham and the three others dropped back into the forest, ran after Tomme and the Invisible People. They knew where to go. To the small river where, just a few days before, the Great Anaconda had swallowed the spirit of Wanadi, and taken it to the dreamlight.

Jabuti said to Tomme, "If we retreat into the forest now, they will never catch us. They will never find us. Let's not risk more deaths."

Caya was still distressed by the killing of Pequi, who had been her friend. She did not yet know of the death of her husband. Tomme watched her, as he crouched by the water. Kachiri was with him. She said, "The women of our tribe have been through a terrible ordeal. We do not seek revenge, but we must make it safe for the Invisible People to live in the World. Now that Jacareh has the fire-weapon, we are not safe. We must not move from this place until it has been done."

"Kachiri speaks for me as well," Tomme said. "For my part, I do not seek revenge either. But if our children are to live long enough to undergo their hunt-deaths, then we must rid the World of an Indian who carries wilderness weapons. We must wait here. We must fight. The Great Ones will decide which of us will live and which of us will die."

Markham watched his son with pride. The conversation among the Indians had been fast, and he had missed much of it. But he had grasped enough of what was being said to appreciate that what would happen, now, would be a final confrontation. Within a few hours, one of the two unknown tribes of the *makira aku* would no longer exist. But the extinction would have been chosen by the tribes themselves.

The Fierce Ones came an hour later. First there was the hissing. Then silence. Then the disturbance in the middle canopy, across the river. Then the air filled with the silent wind of blow-pipe darts, and Jabuti's son, Wishah, was struck in the chest, and died.

A moment later, automatic weapon fire brought a stream of glowing tracer across the river and clattering into the forest. Jacareh stormed across the water, his warriors beside him. There was a Brazilian trader with them as well, and the man saw Markham and fired.

Markham fired back. The trader vanished into the flowing water and was carried away. Jacareh shot a short burst of fire, then reeled backwards as Jabuti's shotgun roared. But the chieftain of the Fierce People was not killed; he staggered and kept on coming.

Arrows and darts whistled through the night air. But it was the Fierce Hunters who fell, one after another, the survivors soon scattering back into the forest.

Mapi raced after them, splashing through the water, shrieking, "You are not fierce! You are not fierce!"

Tomme called him back, shouted to him to keep his body low. Mapi returned across the river, looking abashed. Tomme said, "There is no need to risk your life unnecessarily."

Mapi understood. "I know. The women need me alive."

Tomme pushed him back into cover, where the others were now hiding. All but Markham. He was on his belly by the river, his rifle held in front of him. Tomme ran, crouched low, and dropped down next to his ghost father.

"Where is Jacareh?" Tomme asked.

"Just what I was asking myself," Markham said. "He was hit in the arm, but he kept coming. Then he vanished. I don't think he's dead. But I didn't see him retreating with the others."

Tomme looked nervously behind him. "The other Fierce Ones have fled. They are dead, now. Their spirits have deserted them. But not Jacareh. He is the great jaguar. He has too much pride, too much power."

"I kind of agree," Markham muttered in English, then approximated a translation for his son, adding, "Let's get out of here."

They ran through the forest, silent and fast. In single file they wound their way towards the hunt-trail that led from the edge of the World to the place of the burnt village of the Invisible People. Markham ran at the rear, carrying his rifle. Mapi ran at the front, stabbing and thrusting at the shadows, occasionally whispering his war cry. He had killed his first man, tonight, and the blood fever was high in him. Tomme had seen this, and it did not please him.

When they had run for a few hours they stopped, and grouped in a part of the forest that was not a clearing, but which was less tangled than usual. Caya was still mourning for Pequi, and Kachiri comforted her. Jabuti was mourning for his own son. Everyone was hungry, now, but they felt safe.

Tomme said, to his father, "You must return to the city. Thank you, father, for helping us become a people again."

Markham realized that for the first time Tomme had called him "father," and not "ghost father."

"I will come further with you, if you want."

"No. We must go on. And you must go back. In years to come we will tell our children of you."

Markham suddenly felt distressed. Again he had encountered his son, and again it was a time of parting. Part of him desperately wanted to run on with them, at least as far as the dam. Part of him knew that Tomme's words must be obeyed.

Jabuti said, "With the fire-weapons we can defend ourselves for a while."

But Tomme took the shotgun from him. Jabuti gasped his objection. When Tomme held out his hand to Jabuti's surviving son, Gnaru, the younger man passed the automatic pistol to him. Tomme said, "Now you are the kin of the Invisible People. We will use arrows, spears and blow-pipes, not the fire-weapons." He passed the guns to Markham, who took them from him. Still talking to the others, Tomme said, "Go ahead. Mapi, lead the way. I shall follow."

When they were alone, Tomme said, "Father, look after my mother, always remind her that I have her in my heart, and that I have her heart with me . . ." he patted the pouch, where the moth, whether dead or alive, still remained.

"I shall, Tomme. Don't worry." He felt a sudden despair, a sense of anger that Tomme's life would probably be so short, and was likely to end painfully. He said, "Do you remember where we ate our meal, when you first met the Invisible People?"

Tomme said, "I remember a man running into the World. He was waving his arms like a bird. He was shouting, but there seemed to be no sound. He never seemed to reach the World, even though he was running as hard as he could towards it." Tomme paused. "I have dreamed of this man for many hunt-trails. The man is you, father. Perhaps it was the last thing I saw of you before Wanadi carried me home."

Markham swallowed hard. *Tommy had been there even when he and Jean had entered the forest! They had not seen him! They had been unable to see him!*

He said, "There is a great stone wall there, now. It stands across the river—"

"The log jam," Tomme said. "I saw it when we came in pursuit of the Fierce Ones. It is a frightening thing."

"It is a very frightening thing," Markham agreed. "It stops the river flowing as it once did. Because of the log jam there will be a great invasion of the Termite People into the World. They will enter the World and destroy it for the precious things that it contains. Tomme, your time in the World will be very short. For every building like the one where the women were held, there will soon be a thousand. For every Indian like Jacareh, there will soon be a thousand. They will chase the Great Ones from the World, and they will destroy the villages of people like your people."

Tomme shook his head. "They will not find us. We *are* the Invisible People. We will always be in the World. Even though you believe we are not there, that we have gone . . . *we will be there*. You will just not see us."

"The log jam creates power. The people who come to use that power will see everything."

Tomme saw his father's sadness, his despair. He said, "Father, if that is a log jam, water can break it. Water breaks even the best log jams that my people can make."

"But this is a *great* log jam."

"Then it will take a *great* flood of water to break it!" He grinned. "When we wish it to rain we sing to the frogs. We will sing very loudly, this time. We will gather a *big* rain."

Markham smiled. "I shall sing a little song myself." He reached out and hugged Tomme. "Goodbye, Tomme. Again. Stay invisible."

"You will always be able to see me, father. I shall never be invisible to you."

Markham slipped away, back towards the outpost building, near to which he had hidden the car.

Tomme picked up his bow—he had no arrows—and his blow-pipe. He had a single dart in his belt. He drew it out and held it with the pipe, then turned to follow Mapi and the others.

After a few minutes he stopped and listened. There was movement ahead of him, but not the movement he would have expected from the rest of his tribe. It sounded like a monkey, furtively moving through the low brush.

Either that or a cat, slinking towards him.

Tomme felt startled. He probably had the smell of blood on him. The cat had noticed it and was approaching him cautiously. Even though he was a tall human, and the cats usually avoided humans, the blood smell would have aroused the animal's appetite.

Tomme placed the last dart into his blow-pipe. He held the blow-pipe horizontally and advanced through the darkness, his eyes wide, trying to see by the faint light of a small moon and the scattering of stars.

He entered a clearing. He stopped at the edge, warily watching the darkness ahead of him. And the cat stepped out to meet him. It was grinning. It walked on its hind legs.

Its name was Jacareh.

Jacareh laughed. He held his gun in one hand, pointing it at Tomme. His other arm hung limp by his side. Around his neck he carried one of the black boxes that Markham had called a "bullet clip." Tomme knew that it was these which contained the fire that roared.

He swung up his pipe. There was no time to think, or to react, all he could do was fight. Jacareh screeched with pleasure and a brief burst of fire spat from the gun towards Tomme. Tomme had realized that it would come and he flung himself to one side. As he did so, he dropped the pipe, and the poisoned dart fell free.

Jacareh exploded with laughter. He walked into the clearing. The moon made his white and red face glow like an evil, insect's mask.

"I am Jacareh. I am the jaguar. I am the leader of the Fierce People."

Tomme said, "I am Tomme, son of Wanadi. I am the leader of the Invisible People."

Jacareh bowed slightly, still grinning. "I shall eat you, every bit of you, because the Invisible People are sweet to the taste."

"If you eat me I shall haunt you from your belly. Always. You shall never eat without pain."

Jacareh didn't like that. He looked angry, then scowled. He pushed the gun towards Tomme and aimed carefully. Then he fired.

No fire spat. No voice roared.

For a moment the two men stared at each other. Then Tomme realized what it meant. The fire was gone. Jacareh would have to replace the fire in the gun. Jacareh knew this too. He dropped to one knee, rested the gun across his leg and began to struggle with the empty fire-box.

Tomme flung himself towards his blow-pipe, fumbling in the darkness to find it. Jacareh had the fire-box free and had ripped the new one from around his neck. He shouted at Tomme, roared like an animal.

Tomme couldn't find the dart! He banged his hand around the ground, fearful of impaling himself upon his own poison. Jacareh rammed the new fire-box into the gun.

Tomme found his dart and pushed it into the pipe. He swung the pipe round and blew hard. Jacareh squeezed the trigger on the M16 and fire roared, it roared long and loud, up into the canopy, up among the stars, bright lights in the heavens, shattering and clattering through the tree tops.

When the fire was finished, still Jacareh stood, the gun raised above his head. Tomme's dart quivered in his neck, the poison deep in his system, draining the life from him.

He dropped to his knees, his arm falling. He stared at Tomme and sighed. But he remained kneeling. He remained alive.

Mapi burst from the forest into the clearing and raised his spear to finish the life of Jacareh forever.

"We will burn him, and eat him!" Mapi shouted.

"No!" Tomme said loudly. Spear raised, Mapi hesitated, then said, "It is what he has done to so many of our people! It will be a good revenge."

"No . . ." Tomme repeated, more softly.

He approached Jacareh. The Fierce Hunter could not move. He watched Tomme bitterly, and then the look softened, became remorseful. "The Fierce Ones are no more," he whispered. "You have won a great fight. Now you are the only True People."

"We have always been the Invisible People," Tomme said. "There are many people in the forest, and those who are true to the forest are the True People."

Jacareh tried to wave him quiet, but he was too drained, too weakened by the poison. Mapi shifted restlessly from foot to foot, his spear still ready to strike, anxious for another kill.

Jacareh said, "I ask to die as one of you. Set my soul free with fire. Add a few ashes of my bones to the dust of those who went before you. Perhaps a little of my Fierceness will be of help in years to come."

Mapi smiled enthusiastically and looked at Tomme.

"No." Tomme said.

Jacareh, failing fast, whispered, "Please . . ."

Tomme crouched before him; repeated, "No, Jacareh. We have no need of your Fierceness. Already in our people we have that Fierceness now. But I shall tell stories of you to my children. They will always know of Jacareh, the leader of the Fierce Ones."

Jacareh nearly smiled. He seemed content. He said, "Yes. That will be good. Jacareh, who has the heart of the Jaguar."

But Tomme shook his head. "Jacareh, who has the skin of a Jaguar, but the heart of a tame white pig!"

"No!" Jacareh shouted. The word emerged as a rasping hiss. Then he grimaced, rolled up his eyes, and died. Tomme helped his body to rest. He stood up and turned to Mapi. "We will leave him here. The carrion-eaters will reclaim their own."

Mapi didn't understand why Tomme had done this. "We have need of his fierceness. Why did you deny him?"

"Because there is one coming to the Invisible People who already has all the fierceness of Jacareh's tribe."

"Who?" Mapi asked excitedly.

Tomme smiled at his old friend, but there was a great sadness in his eyes and the smile was wistful. "He is close to us, Mapi. Every day that passes brings him closer still. I had not really understood it until now."

"When he comes," Mapi said, "I want to be by your side to greet him."

"Don't talk about it now," Tomme said. "There are other things to do."

Mapi agreed. He thrust his spear twice towards the dead Jacareh, then followed Tomme in search of the others.

6

From his office in the AmazCo Tower, Bill Markham watched the rain lashing against the windows and drenching the city. The downpour was so heavy that his room—now nearly cleared of his belongings—was dark. He couldn't see the river, or the apartment block where he lived. The sky was grey with the sheeting, relentless water.

Behind him the door opened and Enrico Costa walked quickly into the office. He looked at the packing-cases and the suddenly bare walls.

"It won't be the same without you, Bill."

Markham turned from the window and smiled. "I'll miss you too, Enrico. Some storm, huh?"

"You'd better come with me," Costa said. "It's more of a storm than you think. There's a massive cloud build-up . . . right over the dam, and up-water of the dam."

Costa's voice was edgy. The little man seemed very anxious, and Markham followed him briskly through the building to the video room. Here, all the monitors were displaying satellite views of the Yuruan river system, and there were feverish discussions going on around each of them. Markham leaned close to the latest satellite view and let his breath whistle slowly through his teeth.

Costa was right. The storm clouds were huge, a great swirl on the map, completely obliterating the view of the dam, and its river-feed.

"We've never seen anything like it," Costa said. "It caught the weather people by surprise."

"When did it start to build up?"

"Yesterday," Costa said. "The storm clouds just seemed to appear above the forest, then move into this location and just sit there, slowly building. It doesn't move."

"How's the rain below it?"

"Light at the moment. But when the storm breaks, a lot of water is going to hit that dam."

Markham watched the monitor screen for a moment more, then straightened up, looking pale. "The Indians call it a 'big rain,' " he said to Costa.

"The Indians can call it what they like. We call it trouble."

"You may be right. Let's go take a look."

By the time they reached the site of the dam, Costa's "light rain" had changed in character. The helicopter battled through fierce winds and driving rain to make a safe landing on the pad. It was immediately battened down. Markham ran to the engineering offices, hardly able to see through the torrential downpour. It was after dark, and the site was illuminated by huge arc-lights, but these seemed dim and faint in the swirl of water.

As he reached the offices, Costa in full pursuit, he turned and quickly glanced up at the towering, curved face of the dam. It was finished, an impressive, arc-lit structure that looked solid and unmovable. It would stand for ever. Not even a big rain would bring it down.

"Look!" Costa shouted through the downpour. He was pointing to the tarmac road that led away to the strip mines.

The road was alive with frogs.

Once inside, Costa and Markham took stock of matters with Joseph Perrera. Water had jumped between the Yuruan and Pirikatu systems at two points. The Yuruan itself had risen by ten feet in the last forty minutes.

Perrera said, "But the dam *will* hold!" It was part question, part statement.

Markham said, "No point in taking chances. I've never seen or heard of rain like this. We could have a problem."

"What sort of problem?" Perrera asked stiffly.

"Even a flood-over is going to be dangerous. So get the men off the dam, and off the mining strips. Get them to higher ground."

Perrera was pale. He looked very angry. "What about your safety margin, Bill? You calculated that nothing could bring your concrete wall down . . ."

Markham met his cold gaze with equal cool. "I could have been wrong," he said. "My calculations could have been wrong."

"You mean the dam might not hold."

"I mean I don't see the point in taking chances. Get the place evacuated before the big water hits."

"There are a thousand men out there!" Perrera shouted.

"Then get going!" Markham shouted back. "A precautionary measure, Joseph. Just a precautionary measure."

Are you singing for the rain, Tomme? Is it you who's doing this?

Markham ran quickly along a catwalk, towards the small hut marked "explosives." He carried a torch. Around him, and below him, the lights were winking out and the ground was alive with cars and trucks taking the men to safety.

Then the dam lights themselves went out and Markham was in darkness, the rain sheeting against him as he slipped and slid his way to the hut.

I must be out of my mind. This is madness. Ten years to build the dam . . . *my* dam. So I'll damn well do as I please.

He unlocked the door to the explosives hut and slipped inside. He gathered up the equipment he needed, then went back out into the storm and began to make his way down to one of the low stress-points on the dam structure.

My little bit to help the forest. They can always build another log jam. They have the money.

Lightning flashed above him and thunder growled from the rolling blackness of the clouds. In the distance there was another sound, a deeper, more frightening vibration.

The big water was coming.

He backed off from the base of the dam, stumbling in the darkness, eyes alert for guards, or sheltering workers. But everyone had fled the site and he was quite alone. He unreeled the electrical wire connecting the charges with the small detonator that he had slung round his neck. The distant booming sound grew stronger. He could imagine what the river looked like on the other side of the dam . . . a wide flood, with an approaching wave hundreds of feet high. It would be ripping away trees and soil, smashing them from the earth with all the ease of a bulldozer.

But his dam would hold against it. He had built it that way. He would give the Great Anaconda a little help.

He quickly attached the wires to the detonator box. A red light winked on, indicating that everything was ready. He cowered on the dam overlook, huddled in his oilskin, protecting the detonator with his body. The roaring of the water became deafening and the whole ground seemed to shake.

A moment later the wave rose above the dam like a huge whale rising from the sea, a sinister leviathan towering into the black sky, hesitating, then crashing down and over the dam. An immense arm of water came flooding across the overlook and Markham flung himself back into what cover he could find, slipping as he did so. He fell on the detonator and depressed the handle. But as he scrambled away from the crashing waves, he saw that one of the wires had come loose.

Hauling himself up on to a railing, he stood watching as the curved wall of the dam bulged, then slowly subsided, concrete blocks the size of houses sinking to the ground and being flung across the flimsy portakabins by the flood tide that followed. For a second Markham was too shocked, and too awed to move. He just watched the river take away the marks of man, sweeping through the mining site, a sheet of water that moved like a great silver snake, and crushed the world before it.

Then he flung the detonator out into the flood, out into the darkness.

There would be an investigation, of course. Perrera would suspect sabotage and Markham would support him in that suspicion. The evidence was all washed away, all the evidence that might implicate Markham himself. And of course, if sabotage was accepted then his belief in the strength of the dam would be vindicated.

It was that belief, however, which he now found confusing. *Had* he blown a weak point in the structure? Or had the wire been disconnected before detonation, making his sabotage useless? In which case—how had the dam broken? In his heart he *knew* that the dam should have stood even the most powerful flood wave.

He had calculated the strength of the structure based on the most impossible water flow. This storm was amazing, but it was just a storm! The dam should have held.

Unless something else had been in the water. Unless something else had breached the log jam, something that had then turned back, perhaps—or slipped through with the flood unseen.

Something like . . .

But he had no idea what it might have been. It was just fancy. Like it was fancy to assume that his son, in the forest, had called the storm clouds, singing the song of the big rain. It was a freak of atmosphere, that was all. A terrible, destructive freak of atmosphere.

In any case, they could build the next dam without him.

EPILOGUE

There was one story which came to him in a dream, not as a remembered image from his childhood.

One summer (he had dreamed) the Edge of the World, which for so long had been coming closer to their village, began to grow further away. A hunter visited the place of the ruined log jam and saw how that wilderness was now a small forest. The machines that had eaten the Grandfather trees were silent. Their color had changed from the yellow of the sunflower to the red-brown of earth.

Wherever the hunters of the Invisible People went, in this dream, they found only silence in the wilderness, and the Edge of the World growing farther from them. Among the new trees were the ruined huts of the Termite People, and for a long time these were held in fear, in case the ghosts still lived in them.

But for some reason—perhaps because there was better hunting elsewhere in the wilderness—even the ghosts had gone.

EMBASSY FILMS ASSOCIATES

presents

THE EMERALD FOREST

Starring

POWERS BOOTHE MEG FOSTER

CHARLEY BOORMAN DIRA PAES

RUI POLONAH CLAUDIO MORENO

TETCHIE AGBAYANI PAULO VINICIUS

EDUARDO CONDE ESTEE CHANDLER

Screenplay By

ROSPO PALLENBERG

Co-Produced By

MICHAEL DRYHURST

Executive Producer

EDGAR F. GROSS

Produced and Directed

by

JOHN BOORMAN

POSTSCRIPT:
Making John Boorman's *The Emerald Forest*

He was seven years old when he disappeared from the Amazon damsite where his father, an American construction engineer, was at work. One moment, the boy was playing in the undergrowth which formed a fringe around the freshly cleared land. A split second later, there was no one there.

For ten years, the father spent every spare moment searching for his son. But when they met again, the boy knew only one father, the chief of the primitive Indian tribe called the "Invisible People." The stranger who faced him, stirring memories of another life, was a "termite man" from the "dead world" beyond the edge of the forest, one of the intruders who chewed down the "grandfather" trees and changed the flow of rivers.

Their reunion begins the adventure of John Boorman's *The Emerald Forest*. "When father and son recognize each other, ten thousand years of human progress separate them," says Boorman. "Does blood, kin, reach across that divide?"

According to the *Los Angeles Times* (October 8, 1972) it does, but only briefly. That report, by correspondent Leonard Greenwood, describes the abduction—and reunion—on which Boorman based his film.

The actual father was a Peruvian whose son, Ezequiel, was kidnapped by Indians who attacked the family campsite along Peru's Javari Mirim River.

During the next decade, the Peruvian ventured deeper and deeper into the Amazon wilderness, in search of wandering tribes which might have encountered his son. Finally he learned that the warlike

Mayurunas had carried out several raids at about the time of the kidnapping.

Hacking his way into the jungle, through rain-swollen, insect-infested swamps and foliage so rampant that "working every daylight hour, he was fortunate to make half a mile a day," he came to a Mayuruna outpost. When he told the tribe's sentries that he would like to speak to their chief, the report continues, "he was taken through the forest to a hunting camp.

"As the chief approached, the father saw that he was surprisingly tall . . . with features which set him apart from the other tribesmen. When the father addressed him in Indian dialect, the youth replied in broken Spanish.

"The father now realized that, despite the tribal markings tattoed in blue dye on the chief's skin, he was talking to his own son."

Memories returned, but "the boy now considered the Indians his people and would not leave the tribe."

The father was certain he would not see his son again. To his amazement, though, the youth suddenly appeared at his parents' home. There he described his life in the jungle, and asked for his father's help to protect his people from their enemies—much as the boy "Tomme" asks for help from Bill Markham in Boorman's screen version.

Like much of Boorman's best work, including *Deliverance* and *Excalibur*, the new adventure pits modern man against the relentless forces of nature. To experience those forces, in terms of his story, Boorman went straight to the source—the Amazon.

Contacting noted Brazilian anthropologist Orlando Villas-Boas, he arranged to be introduced to an Indian tribe of the upper Xingu region—an area whose impenetrable terrain has kept its inhabitants almost totally isolated from the modern world.

After decades of exploitation, the Indians of the area were wary of white men. The tribe had come to trust Villas-Boas because of his efforts to protect the Xingu territory from the greed of ranchers, hunters, and prospectors. But Boorman had to prove himself—and be formally invited.

He succeeded by telling them what his film was about. "The rain forest is threatened by the construction of a huge dam, which will flood vast areas and stop the flow of the river. It forces two tribes away from their home, and brings tragedy to the white dam-builder and his son. What happens shows the difference between living in harmony with nature and exploiting it.

"If the story is good, it will be seen by millions of people. To tell it right, I have to be there. I have to touch the past."

He not only received his invitation, but came as the guest of the wise and friendly Takuma, shaman (or witch doctor) of the Kamaira tribe of the Xingu.

"He asked what I did in my world," says Boorman, recalling a conversation with Takuma, "which is not an easy question to answer to someone who has never seen a movie or a television program. I explained how we stage a scene, then stop, then stage another scene, so as to create a series of illusions.

"I told him, 'It is like a dream.' Then he understood. 'Ah,' he said, 'you do the same work that I do.' "

Following instructions to take nothing with him except a hammock (which he would leave as a present), soap and matches, and a fishing net, Boorman and his guide, anthropologist Maureen Bisilliat, flew as far as possible into the interior of the jungle. They then hiked the rest of the way to the village of the Kamaira.

What Boorman saw—and later recorded in his diary—was "the world at its beginning. There are barbed thorns, spiked leaves, resins that burn, poisonous fruits, grasses that clutch you, huge ants that sting like snakes, caterpillars whose hair raises welts on your skin, tarantulas a foot across wearing 'mink coats'."

Despite such obstacles, Boorman agrees with author/explorer Geoffrey Lean, who calls the rain forest "the most exuberant celebration of life ever to have existed on earth." He shares Lean's view that as "home to half of all living species on earth, it is a biological powerhouse."

The encroachment of civilization and concrete into this realm has disturbing implications, which are a focus of Boorman's film. He notes that "the Amazon rain forest is considered by scientists to provide as much as 35% of the world's oxygen supply through photosynthesis. As mankind moves in, destroying the delicate eco-balance, the climate of our planet . . . in the not so distant future . . . is in danger."

In *The Emerald Forest*, Bill Markham comes to appreciate not only the Indian way of life but also the fact that he is an interloper. "Through his experience with the 'Invisible People,' " says Boorman, "he realizes that it was his own thoughtless blundering into someone else's world that precipitated his personal tragedy. By taking the land of the 'Fierce People,' he set in motion the events that would ultimately cost him his son.

"In one of my earlier films, *Deliverance*, four city men sealed their fate when they came to an Appalachian village and crassly insulted those who lived there. That, too, was a metaphor for our insensitivity to nature."

The first Kamaira Boorman met—warriors returning from fishing—were naked but heavily painted, with eyes that were "strange . . . seeking, probing, open and innocent, yet infinitely mysterious." They carried bows, feathered arrows and harpoon-like spears.

They knew of Maureen Bisilliat, of course, but asked her about her companion. After describing who Boorman was (in the Kamaira dialect), she cautioned him not to reveal the fact that he was the father of twins, since the Kamaira consider twins unlucky.

Once Boorman's gifts were accepted and he had hung his hammock in the designated spot in the shaman's house—a thatched dome 90 feet long, 40 feet wide, and 30 feet high, shared by ten families—the filmmaker was able to observe the tribal lifestyle.

"Their relationships were relaxed, non-monogamous and non-competitive. Men had as many wives as they could care for, and the children were raised by the entire tribe.

"Their daily routine has gone unchanged for hundreds of centuries," he goes on. "The women go off to the manioc patches, returning with heavy roots which look like turnips. They spend hours scraping, boiling and grinding them into flour from which they make a kind of tortilla, setting the juice aside for a delicious sweet soup. The men supplement the diet by fishing in the river.

"Much of the time is occupied by making ornaments from feathers, necklaces from seeds, and paint from bark, berries, and powdered gems with which they decorate themselves in elaborate patterns."

Such markings are important to them. It is part of their other lives, the mystical world whose rituals they cannot perform unless they are properly anointed. To be without paint is to be naked . . . an affront to the spirits.

"This is the soul of their existence . . . to be one with nature," says Boorman.

"We assume that because the Indians of the Amazon are technically ten thousand years in the past, they are primitive in every way," he observes. "Yet they exist on a spiritual level as beautiful and spellbinding as any fantasy any filmmaker has ever conceived. It is in dreams, myths, and visions that their 'real' lives are played out."

He was pleased, therefore, to be invited to join Takuma and his warriors on a journey to find logs for the "Quarup," their ceremony for the dead.

Six perfect logs were needed, to house the temporarily buried bodies of six who had died during the year. Each tree trunk would be decorated, and the ceremony would release the souls to the stars, after which the bodies would be burned, and the ashes poured into a huge urn, thereby joining the ashes of their forebears.

While Boorman could help hunt for the logs, he could not witness the sacred ceremony because he wore clothes. But it convinced him to include a similiar scene in *The Emerald Forest*—and to film it from the point of view of the kidnapped young American, Tommy Markham, who has grown into manhood as the chief's heir.

After ten years of searching for his lost son and finally finding him, Bill Markham must resign himself to the fact that Tommy is lost to him forever. The youngster cannot leave his people. His father, though remembered with love, is now his "Ghost Father" from the "Dead World" beyond the forest's edge. His Indian father, Wanadi, is his true parent. To Boorman, such a decision was perfectly rational.

So pervasive is the spirituality surrounding the Xingu Indians that he refused to use any of them in his film. "While they would have been wonderful actors," he explains, "the filmmaking process would have been totally destructive to their culture."

Instead, he spent four extra months working with detribalized Indians, helping them re-create their lost heritage for *The Emerald Forest*.

It was a small enough offering to appease the powers of the Amazon.